WHAT MY HEART
WANTS TO TELL

WHAT MY HEART
WANTS TO TELL

Verna Mae Slone

THE UNIVERSITY PRESS OF KENTUCKY

Publication of this volume was made possible in part by a grant
from the National Endowment for the Humanities.

Scholarly publisher for the Commonwealth,
serving Bellarmine University, Berea College, Centre College of Kentucky,
Eastern Kentucky University, The Filson Historical Society, Georgetown College,
Kentucky Historical Society, Kentucky State University, Morehead State University,
Murray State University, Northern Kentucky University, Transylvania University,
University of Kentucky, University of Louisville, and Western Kentucky University.
All rights reserved.

Editorial and Sales Offices: The University Press of Kentucky
663 South Limestone Street, Lexington, Kentucky 40508-4008
www.kentuckypress.com

Library of Congress Cataloging-in-Publication Data

Slone, Verna Mae, 1914–
What my heart wants to tell.
Reprint. Originally published: Washington: New Republic Books, 1979.
Includes index.
1. Slone, Verna Mae, 1914–   2. Knott County (Ky.)—Biography.
3. Sloan family. 4. Knott County (Ky.)—Social life and customs. I. Title.
[F457.K5S58 1987]   976.9'165040924 [B]   87-23046
ISBN-10: 0-8131-1634-1
ISBN-10: 0-8131-0174-3 (pbk.)
ISBN-13: 978-0-8131-0174-3 (pbk.)

This book is printed on acid-free recycled paper meeting
the requirements of the American National Standard
for Permanence in Paper for Printed Library Materials.

Manufactured in the United States of America.

 Member of the Association of
American University Presses

For Sarah Jane Owens Slone and Isom B. (Kitteneye) Slone
—My father and mother

ACKNOWLEDGMENTS

THIS BOOK WAS written to honor my father. I loved him so much that I was not willing to let the memory of him die. I would have loved him even if he had not been my father. He is only one of many mountain people—proud, brave, sturdy, hard-working, god-fearing, and sensitive—living in a place and time so unique and different that its very simplicity is too profound to be fully understood and explained.

Also, I hope to dispel some of the myths and misunderstandings of these people soon to be forgotten.

Without God's help, I could never have written these things of my heart.

BIRTH DATES

Isom B. Slone	Feb. 27, 1863 (dec.)
Sarah Jane Slone	April 25, 1872 (dec.)
Flora Belle Slone	Dec. 23, 1888 (dec.)
Frank Morrell Slone	Mar. 7, 1890 (dec.)
Arminda Slone	May 26, 1892 (dec.)
Vince Slone	Dec. 10, 1895
Jezzie Ann Slone	Sept. 4, 1897 (dec.)
Lorenda Slone	Oct. 7, 1899
Devada Slone	Jan. 10, 1902
Lou Frances Slone	Jan. 26, 1904 (dec.)
Edna Earl Slone	Feb. 4, 1906
Sarah Alverta Slone	May 12, 1909 (dec.)
Owen Slone	July 25, 1911 (dec.)
Verna Mae Slone	Oct. 9, 1914

Copied from the old family Bible.
Isom and Sarah were married on July 28, 1887,
by John L. Slone, the brother to Grandpa Jim.

A section of photographs follows page 80.

DEAR GRANDCHILDREN:

I am writing you this letter to be read later when you are older and can understand.

If you are the kind of folks who honor money and prestige, then I have very little to leave you: just a few handmade quilts and a few old silver coins, made and collected over my sixty years of life—not much to show for a lifetime of hard work. But I hope by writing this book, I can pass on to you the heritage my father left me.

Materialwise, he only gave me an acre of land, half of a house (the other half had been torn down), a few handmade chairs, a basket, and less than two hundred dollars in money. But, believe me, I would not exchange the memories I have of him for all the gold in Fort Knox. And the truths and wisdom of life he taught me, have been a staff and a rod to comfort me all the days of my life.

In this book I will try to pass on to you, all my memories of him.

He was a very wonderful man, wise beyond his own place and time, with a spontaneous wit and humor that was "meractious" for his limited education. He was always ready to give his neighbors a helping hand, whether it be to lay the "worm" of a stake and rider fence, square up the foundation of a building, help a sick cow, or prepare the dead for burial.

These stories will probably be like a large ball of string: made up of many small strings too short to use and too long to throw away.

Grandpa Kitteneye had so many sayings—little nuggets of wisdom and philosophy—that contain so much truth and basic principles of life. I shall try to remember and pass them on as I manage to work them into my story. I think his best was "prepare for the worst, expect the best, and then take whatever comes." He not only said this, but he believed it and used it to live by, and taught me to do the same. I have been influenced so much by his thoughts and truths that I sometimes wonder where his thinking leaves off and my own begins.

Grandchildren, this letter is not to be a sermon. In writing this, I will write as I remember it. I may make a few small changes, but basically it's all true.

So many lies and half-truths have been written about us, the mountain people, that folks from other states have formed an image of a gun-totin', "baccer-"spitting, whiskey-drinking, barefooted, foolish hillbilly, who never existed, but was conceived and born in the minds of the people who have written such things as *Stay on Stranger* and the *Beverly Hillbillies*. And as lies seem to be more easily believed than truths, no matter what we do, we can't make folks believe we are any different. These lies and half-truths have done our children more damage than anything else. They have taken more from us than the large coal and gas companies did by cheating our forefathers out of their minerals, for that was just money. These writers have taken our pride and dignity and have disgraced us in the eyes of the outside world. When our children go into the cities for work or are drafted into the army, they are forced to deny their heritage, change their way of talking, and pretend to be someone else, or be made to feel ashamed, when they really have something to be proud of.

God knew that it would take brave and sturdy people to survive in these beautiful but rugged hills. So He sent us His very strongest men and women, people who could enjoy life and search out the few pleasures that were contained in a life of hard work. They were an enduring people, who did not whimper and complain because their burdens were heavy. They loved each other and lived closer to God and nature than any folks anywhere.

So with God's help, I hope my brain can say to my hands what my heart wants to tell.

VERNA MAE SLONE
October 1978

WHAT MY HEART
WANTS TO TELL

CHAPTER ONE

IT WAS SO cold that February morning in 1863, the wind almost bounced off the sides of the hills as it roared its way up Caney Creek and up the mouth of Trace, whirling the icy snow around the log cabin. It was an angry wind that bent its fury against the sturdy logs, trying to find a crack or hole between the wood so as to get to the woman and little seven-year-old boy inside. But the cabin had withstood many such winds. It was built in 1809 by Shady Slone, and was now owned by his grandson Jim Slone. Jim's wife Frankie and ElCaney were safe and warm inside.

Frankie had listened to the winds last night. She had not slept very much. The cabin seemed so empty with only the two of them. She was used to all three beds being full. Her older boys had gone to Walker Town (now Hazard) to swap her hand-tied lace to some salt and coffee.

She laughed at herself when she remembered the coffee and how she had cooked the first batch she had ever seen. The peddler had said, "It's good with fresh meat." And so she had used it as a spice. Of course the meat had to be given to the dogs and they did not like it either.

The wind whistled through the "noise maker," which Jim's great-grandfather had once helped him to make. They had clipped the hairs from a horse's tail and fastened them tightly between the logs, where they were pinned together at the corners of the cabin. The hairs were placed in groups of one, two, and three, and were so arranged that the wind blowing through them made a musical sound. Frankie did not like to listen to the whining, sad, musical tones. It reminded her of death and the scary stories Jim's great-grandmother had told of the "wee folks in Ireland."

Frankie reminded herself she must get up. ElCaney would soon be awake. He had been a little sick all winter, a bad cold that just would not go away. She had made catnip tea several times and ginger tea, adding a little whiskey to the tea, and had rubbed his chest and feet with the juice of a roasted onion. Nothing had seemed to help. The boy said the onion made him stink.

Frankie got up slowly and put her dress on. Going to the hearth with her shoes in her hand, she took the poker and pushed at the "fore log" that was now very near burned in two. By raising first one end and then the other, using the poker as a lever, she pushed the half-burned log back against the "back log" and then placed a fresh log across in front. She counted the logs left in the pile. Only three, but that would be enough; the boys would be home this evening or tomorrow anyway.

She picked up the water bucket and saw that the water had frozen solid.

"Well, it will take too long to melt that," she thought. She slipped her feet into her shoes and reached for an empty bucket. It was her milk bucket, but the cow was dry now, so she could take it and go to the spring for water.

As she raised up, a pain struck her in the back and moved on around in front, down low. She clasped her hands against her body and said, "Oh, no, it can't be that; the baby han't due till April or the first of May. Jest an upset stomach; we've been eating too much of the same thing."

All the "sass" had been gone since just after Christmas and there was no more hog meat, just a few more shucky beans. She wouldn't dare eat any more of the "taters"; they had to be kept for seed.

There was one more shoat to kill. That was why the boys had gone after the salt. She should have killed it in January. "Everybody knowed a hog did not mend any during February," but she had wanted to keep this one until Jim came home. But it did not look like he would come home soon, and if she did not kill the hog now there would not be enough of the cold weather left to cure the meat.

"Well, a good mess of fresh meat shore would taste good, Jim or no Jim."

As she lifted the heavy latch to open the door, she saw a long hickory stick leaning against the side of the house. Nick had cut that the other day for ElCaney to ride as a horse. She took the hickory stick in one hand and the bucket in the other, and using the "horse" as a cane, she braced herself against the wind and started to the spring.

As she looked up she saw a beautiful red bird sitting in a low branch of the "weepin' willer"; she hurriedly repeated, almost without thinking, "I wish the war would soon be over and Jim would be back home." Then she thought, "I wonder how many red birds I have made that same wish on. Well, a red bird shore is a purty thing. I have heard of some people eatin' them. I'd starve 'fore I would."

When she got to the spring, a thin sheet of ice had frozen over the top. She took her stick and tapped lightly on the ice and dipped her bucket in. Turning, she hurried back up the path. She saw that she had forgotten to close the door behind her after she had come out. As she set the bucket of water down on the side of the table, another pain hit her, much harder than the first. And as she grasped the edge of the table for support, she knew she had been fooling herself. It was her time, and the baby was saying, "Here I come, ready or not."

She filled the iron teakettle with water and set it before the fire, off to one side. Here it would soon be warm and out of her way, so she could bake some bread. She thought, "I will need all the strength I can muster, so I won't take time to fix a plum out-and-out mess; I will just make a snack for me and ElCaney."

The thought never entered her mind to be afraid; it was just something that had to be done. "Women were made to bear children; children, the Good Book had said. . . . in pain shall you bear them." Of course she did not enjoy pain, but it was something to be gotten over with. She tried to keep her mind on the great joy she would have when it was over.

She mixed a little cornmeal with a pinch of salt and soda, and mixed it with a little water, making a very thick paste. Then she took a board from behind the wood pile stacked in the corner of the room. This board was about three feet long, eight inches wide, and one inch thick. One side of it had been made very smooth. She placed this board at a forty-degree angle before the fire, propping it up by placing a smaller one behind it.

She divided the cornmeal dough into two patties and placed them on the hot board. On the other end of the board she put two large slices of dried beef, sprinkling them with the last of the salt. Soon the cabin was filled with the smell of food, a good appetizing odor that would have brought water to anyone's mouth.

It wasn't long before ElCaney woke up. "Oh, Maw, I smell

hotcakes and meat, and I shore am hungry."

"Well, jump up, son, and eat. Don't mind putting your shoes on, fer soon as you eat you have to go back to bed."

"Oh, Maw!"

"You know I mean what I say and I say what I mean."

After they had eaten, she made ElCaney go back to bed.

"Turn ye face toward the wall and don't look around till I tell ye," said Frankie.

"But, Maw, why?"

"Do as I say and no 'why' to it." She wished Caney wasn't here; he was too young.

"You know I told you how the ol' Hoot Owl was goin' to bring us another little'un."

"Yeah, but, Maw, you said it would be after we had our corn all dug in, and Maw, it's still winter outside."

"Well, Caney, me or that ol' Hoot Owl, one or t'uther got mistook, fer he is bringin' that young'un now."

Although Caney was only seven, he knew far more about births than his mother realized. A mountain boy lives so close to nature that he learns many things at an early age.

Another pain came so hard and sharp that she sank to the floor, caught her breath, and murmured, "Please God, let me keep my mind, so I can take care of this little'un You're sending me." She realized the baby was being born. She could not even get to the bed, and pulling Caney's pallet before the fire, she braced herself for the coming of her child.

In less than an hour, Caney, still facing the wall, heard a small, weak cry almost like a kitten and he said, "Can I look now, Maw?"

"Now listen, Caney, and listen good. Ye take that hickory stick Nick cut fer ye a hoss and knock down some of them wearin' things hangin' on that 'are pole and ye bring me my underskirt, that white'un, and bring me some twine from that wood box under the bed. And reach me the knife from the table."

"Shore, Maw."

"And hurry, son."

And Caney scrambled from the bed, feeling very important as he got all the things his maw had asked for. Still hearing the small whimpering voice, he could not believe it was a baby's, it was so low and weak.

It seem to him like hours before his mother called him to her side and showed him what she had wrapped in her white underskirt. And when he looked he almost gasped.

"But, Maw, it's so puny."

"Yeah, under three pounds is my guess, but ye know he has this whole big world to grow in. He is almost as small as a kitten."

And ElCaney answered, "Kitten, Maw! Why he han't as big as a kitten's eye."

And that, my dear grandchildren, is how my father became known as Kitteneye. Although the name written in the Good Book was Isom B. Slone, he was to be stuck with the name Kitteneye all his born days.

CHAPTER TWO

So KITTENEYE GREW. Although he was always small in size, he was hard and sturdy as the hills that stood protecting and imprisoning his cabin home at the mouth of Trace on Caney Creek. But he was as gentle as the cool summer winds that found their winding path up the narrow hollow.

He was walking by himself by the time he was seven months old. By his first birthday, he had learned to climb over the four-rail fence and get outside the yard.

I do not know too much about his childhood years, but he was a "smart young'un." I know he learned all the old folks could teach him. From his father he learned how to make the staves that became "picklin' barrels" to hold our sauerkraut, pickles, corn, and beans, and the "water barrels" for water (and I hate to admit it, but sometimes something much stronger). The washtubs and buckets were made from shorter staves. The iron to make the hoops that held the staves together was the only thing that had to be store bought.

Sometimes they used one-half of a log for a wash trough. It could also be used for a water trough for their stock. If they were lucky enough to find a hollow log, so much the better. Then they were saved the trouble of having to hew or burn a trench to hold the water.

Many times they would leave a hollow stump in the yard for the same purpose. They would also chip a deep hole in a stone or rock for a wash basin. These were always smaller and here they washed their hands or face.

Kitteneye must have helped his father to build a "kil," a place to dry apples and peaches. They dug a ditch about three-feet wide and five- or six-feet long. On each side of this hole they put a small wall made from creek rocks, cemented together with clay. A large flat slate rock (or two or three small ones) was used to form a roof. One end of this man-made cave was left open; the other end was finished with more creek rocks and clay, to form a very low chimney. The tablelike top was made smooth with about a two-inch layer of clay. Sometimes they built an open shed with a split board roof, to keep off the rain.

He learned to keep a slow fire burning in the opening on the ground inside the kil, before it was ready for the apples. The rocks and clay had to be slowly "seasoned out," for too much heat would cause the clay to crack or break.

The apples were peeled and quartered, the seeds and core removed. Sometimes they dried apples with the hull on, without removing any of the skin. Other folks preferred the "rung" process: Only a circle of peeling, around the center and another at each end, was taken off, leaving the remaining skin.

There is nothing in the world more tasty than a dried-apple pie. Eaten raw they are a kind of combination bubble gum and candy to nibble on. There were Horse apples, Johnson Winter Keepers, Black Twig, August Arch,

Virginia Beauty, Roman Beauty, Belle Flower, and June Apples. A sweet apple called Rusty Sweet was good for drying, as was the Roman Beauty.

Peaches were also dried, but although the hills were full of wild grapes and plums, I don't think they fooled with these fruits.

From his father Kitteneye learned to split rails and to make a stake and rider fence. It took a very skilled person to lay the "worm," or first row. They would try to follow the ridge, or tops of the hill whenever possible. Sometimes they'd go through a flat, or bench the small level footholds. But how they built the fences strong enough to hold up, when they were following an upgrade of a ninety-degree angle, I can't understand. It would seem as if the first wind would have sent them flying all over the place. But if the "worm" was laid right, the fence usually stood firm and strong until it decayed.

Kitteneye's father also taught him to lay the foundation for a house. It had to be on a "four square" to be solid and strong. The cabins were always low on the ground. This served a double purpose: It was warmer and the last logs didn't have to be lifted so high. The location of the cabin was determined by the closest spring of fresh water, usually in the middle of the only little bottom ground they had. Then the garden, or "truck patch" was planted all around the cabin.

With only a "straight axe" and a "broad axe" for tools, these cabins were built solid and strong, ugly and rough, but so snug and warm—sturdy as the men who were to spend their lives in them.

These mountain home builders had no gadgets to "count off" inches or feet, yet all the logs had to be the same length, and each corner at a forty-five-degree angle. They used the width of their hands for measurement of one foot. The hands placed downwards—open and with spread out thumbs meeting together—was one foot. Of course some folks' hands were larger than others. This was solved by learning just how far to lap your thumbs—to the end of the nail or up to the first knuckle. (Kitteneye's hands were smaller than most, so in order to get a true measurement he had to add the width of one thumb to the width of his hands.) Then they would cut a straight hickory stick to the desired length of several feet, and use the stick for longer measurement. And by placing the heel of one foot before the toe of the other foot, they could "step off" an acre and even miles, and were much more accurate than you would presume.

Kitteneye learned from his folks the different plants, the names and uses of all the trees that grew on the steep hills of Trace, Hollybush, Short Fork, and Bunion. He knew which tree made the best boards or shingles, that the chestnut was the best to use for fence rails because it split easy. The black locust was hard and sturdy and did not rot, so post and foundation logs were cut from these. The birch made good stove wood. Maple burned a lot longer, but the birch gave a pleasant odor when burned. Of course, the pine caught fire more easily, making good kindling and torches. Baskets were made from white oak, chair rounds (rungs) were hickory, the legs maple.

Kitteneye learned that cutting the bark off in a circle around the chestnut tree, about three or four feet from the ground, would cause the tree to die. The best time was in early spring, when the sap was in the tree. That way the wood had a better chance of seasoning or drying out and the tree would be ready for use later. If the tree had been cut down it would have decayed very quickly. There are some large chestnuts still standing on the hill above our house that bear these "rings." I love to think this was the work of my father's hand.

Of course all this work was hard, but to these mountain folks work came as natural as breathing. They loved to work. They began as soon as it was light enough to see, continuing until it was too dark.

Kitteneye's folks taught him about planting, gathering, and putting up food in accordance with the "signs of the seasons," or the signs of the zodiac. They did not use the astrological names, but the parts of the human body that represented each sign: Aires (head); Taurus (neck); Gemini (arms); Cancer (breast); Leo (heart); Virgo (belly, bowels); Libra (kidneys); Scorpio (sex organs); Sagittarius (thighs); Capricorn (knees); Aquarius (legs); Pisces (feet).

There were many rules that went along with the signs:

1. You must not castrate an animal when the sign was in Scorpio.

2. You must not wean a baby when the sign was in the head. If you did, the baby would cry until the sign went out to the feet. Also, you must not wean a calf in this sign.

3. If you planted your cucumbers when the sign was in Gemini, then they would grow two together and produce more. Beans were also planted in this sign so the blooms would not drop off.

4. Sweet potatoes were "set out" or replanted when the sign was in the feet, so they would "take root" better. All plants that were transplanted in this sign grew better. House plants made from "cuttings" should also be started in this sign.

5. You must not have a tooth pulled when the sign is in the head.

There are many, many more. When my father grew up, he did not believe any of these. He said, "I plant my stuff in the ground, not in the moon."

From his mother Kitteneye learned to tell time "by the sun." The length and the direction of the shadow cast by a tree or a large rock would determine the hour of the day.

You had to take into account the time of year, if it was spring, winter, or summer. And Frankie knew the stars in the sky by name, not the names you are familiar with, but the names she had been taught: the Seven Sisters, the Dog stars, and the Twin Brothers.

Because they had no calendars, it was hard for them to keep any kind of record. One thing I love to remember was the way they knew it took the same length of time for their fingernails to grow full length as the pregnancy period of a hog. When their sows got with pig, they would cut with a knife a very small nick or hole just where the nail began. When this small scar grew to the end—about three months, three weeks, and three days—they knew that the baby pigs were due to arrive.

Some folks did not know the months. I know one woman who could not tell you the month in which her children were born, but could always tell you if it was fodder-pulling time, grubbing time, or cold weather.

The way the smoke rose from the chimney meant rain or fair weather. This was not altogether a foolish saying. The heaviness of the air brought on by the moisture in the air caused the smoke to rise straight up or float out. Frankie did not understand the scientific reason for this but she had learned by watching and remembering.

Granny Frankie passed on to Kitteneye a vast store of knowledge of herbs: which ones were good for what ailment or sickness, whether for animal or person, and how to prepare them. Some would be used as a "pollus" and some boiled for tea. Oh how I wished I had paid more attention and learned from him what he learned from her. It was not all foolish.

I do remember a few things: Catnip was used for colds and to make you sleep; peach tree bark for vomiting. The bark of the possum bush (pussy willow) was good for headaches.

I remember my father once said, "I don't believe God would have wasted his time to create any plants or varmit or anything at all if it did not have some use or purpose. Us humans are jest to dumb to know what everything is fer."

I know there were some things that had no sense and were only superstition, like carrying a buckeye in your pocket to cure rheumatism. The buckeye is a brown nut with a yellow circle on one side. It's so named because it looks so much like a male deer's eye. There were a few people who believed in this cure; I know Papa did not. He always said, "The only thing carrying a buckeye will do is make a hole in your pocket." And he would rather have a hole in his pocket than in his head.

Kitteneye's only books were the *Blue-backed Speller* and the Bible. From these he learned to read. His favorite heroes were little David, the one with the slingshot, and a Slone, who held a high position in the English army when they told "them frog eaters a thing or two at the battle of Waterloo." There was also supposed to have been a Slone in the army that helped to win the Revolutionary War. I don't know if either of these Slones were real or not. Kitteneye believed they were.

There have been Slones living on Caney since 1790, when Alice Slone, better known as Little Granny, came from Virginia with her husband and three sons. They had a government grant to several acres of land here in Knott County. Slone could have been the Revolutionary soldier. The three half-grown boys, Shady Hall, Isom Adkins, and Isaac Stephens, weren't his sons, but as their stepfather, he gave them his name. He and Alice had one son, Hi, the only true Slone, and he moved to Texas. Shady Hall Slone married Katy Reynolds. One of their sons, Billie, married Sally Casebolt. They were the parents of Jim Summer Slone, my grandfather.

I love to picture in my mind Little Granny's long journey

from "somewhere in Virginia": all their "worldly goods" on two or more oxen-driven wagons; coops filled with squawking geese, ducks, and chickens; one of the boys herding the milk cow and mule.

What did Alice think when she saw these rocky hills, the new home for her family? They were sturdy stock and sufficient unto themselves. They were the first white people to live on Caney. For over 150 years, the Slones lived, loved, fought, and died undisturbed by the outside world, protected and imprisoned by the hills.

Someone once asked my father how far back he could trace the name Slone, and he answered, "Well, for shore I can only go back to Little Granny Alice," and then with a laugh he finished, "but by the way of one of Noah's sons, we go back to Adam."

There are three different ways of spelling our name: Slone, Sloan, and Sloane. We jokingly say that the richer ones spell it Sloane, the middle class, Sloan, and the poorest, Slone. The Slones resent having it spelled Sloan. I know for sure that a man who used an "e" lost many votes in an election on Caney because he had changed the way he spelled his name. It is his privilege to spell his name however he wants to, but it is our privilege to resent it.

I am glad that I did not have to change my name when I got married—although me and my husband are not cousins—and could pass on to my children the name my father gave me. As all my children were boys, all my grandchildren are also Slones. But now that one of my granddaughters is married, there is the first break in the chain.

CHAPTER THREE

IT WAS LATE May in the year 1872. It had been raining almost all morning, but now, about ten o'clock, the sun was trying to shine.

It had rained a lot this spring, and many of the folks up and down Trace were far behind with their corn planting.

Jim was down with the "rumatis" again, and Frankie and the boys were thinking about having a "working," if it ever cleared up enough. They did not like to ask other folks to help them, when everyone's corn was just as weedy, but maybe they would have to.

Kitteneye sat in the open door where the sun came slanting in. The warm sun felt good on his back. All the other boys and the two girls were pulling sprouts, the young shoots that came up around the stumps in the new ground. But Kitteneye had a sore throat. His mother came to the door and looked outside, anxiously scanning the sky.

"Well, the rain's over. Begin 'fore seven, quit 'fore eleven," she said, more to herself than to the small boy.

Then her eyes turned up the hollow. She saw someone walking slowly down the side of the creek—a woman with a bundle in her arms. When she saw the woman slow down as she approached the gate, she knew she was going to have a welcome visitor.

"Well, I do declare, here comes Cindy with the young'un. First time I've seen her out of the holler since last summer."

Kitteneye got up and pulled his chair out of the door, making room for her to enter.

"Come on in, Cindy, shore glad to see ye, and ye bring ye young'un. I been aiming to come up to see it before now, but with one thing and another, I jest kep' putting it off. Here, Kitteneye, give Cindy a chair."

"Yeah, I shore am out of breath. This child is a heavy'un to tote so fer." She sat down as she spoke.

"Here, give me ye bonnet and I'll put it here on the bed." Cindy pulled off her bonnet and used it for fanning her face. "Well, let me see if this one looks like all the rest." Frankie took the baby and unwrapped its bundle. "My land's sake, its almost growed up already. Look here, Kitteneye, look how purty."

Kitteneye gave a shy look and reached for the baby. Taking it gently in his arms, he placed it on the bed and sat down beside it.

"Well, you puny agin, Isom?" Cindy asked.

"Yeah," his mother said, not giving him time to answer for himself. "The palate of his mouth is falling down again. He's allus having trouble that 'er way."

"I heard tell that it was a present cure, if'n you tie ye sock around ye neck and sleep with it on." Cindy was fanning away as she talked.

"I already done that," Kitteneye spoke from the bed. "Maw pulled my ears and my hair straight up. She'll have me bald 'fore I get growed up."

"Jim feeling puny agin?" Cindy asked.

"Yeah, down with the rumatis. Nothin' does him a bit of good. He carried a buckeye in his pocket and turned his shoes with the bottoms up under his bed every night, but he aches and pains. This rain spell makes it worse."

"Oh, Maw, ye know Paw always gets better after we'uns get the corn laid by," Kitteneye laughed.

"Ye better'n let ye paw hear ye say that, he'll whup the hide off'n ye."

"Well, Maw, ye know everbidy says Paw jest has the rumatis in the summer. That's why they call him Jim Summer."

"It don't aggravate ye paw none to be called Jim Summer." Then turning to her visitor she asked, "What brings ye out in this here bad weather?" She wanted to keep Kitteneye from saying more about his father.

"Well, I wanted to see if'n ye could spare me some cabbage plants. Mine did not do one bit of good this year. They jest spindled and died soon as they come up."

"I got a'plenty. Already set out all I want. Ye can have all the rest of the bed, fer as I care. This is a good time to set 'em out. It's been raining; the ground's good and wet. Ye won't have to water 'em none hardly a'tall." Frankie reached for her own bonnet hanging from a nail behind the door.

Cindy put her bonnet back on and answered, "Well, I don't know if the sign's right or not, but I guess if'n I want any sauerkraut fer this winter I better git some cabbage plants in the ground."

"Well, I never thunk it mattered much where the sign was when ye sat 'em out. It all depended on when ye planted the seed. I heard tell if'n ye made kraut, when the sign was in the bowels, it would smell awful." As they started out the door toward the garden, Frankie looked over her back and cautioned Kitteneye.

"Ye stay with the baby while we go pull up them cabbage

plants. Be shore and don't leave it fer one minute, fer that old cat might climb up in the bed and take its breath."

"Shore, Maw, I know."

The two women walked off the porch and through the yard toward the garden.

"I see ye got a right smart of beans planted, got a sight of blooms on 'em. It will be a caution of beans ye'll have, if'n the blooms don't fall off too soon," Cindy remarked.

"Yeah," Frankie answered. "Cindy, I know ye have somp'um a'bearing on ye mind. What is it?"

They had been good friends and neighbors for years and could speak frankly with each other.

"Well, it's what happened yesterday. I 'speck ye knowed that Vince's paw had come back on the creek?"

"Yeah, I knowed, I seed him go up the holler yesterday mornin'."

"Well," Cindy went on, "he come up to our house. Quick as I seed him, I knowed who it was. He had been gone for a long time, but I knowed it was Grandpa Reece soon as I laid eyes on him. Vince takes after his paw a lot. He axed where Vince was and I told him he had took all the big young'uns way back up thar in the last flat to rake weeds. I told him to come in and sit a spell, but he said how he 'spected he would go find Vince. I axed him if he knowed the way and he said he had not fergitten the lay of the land. He kep' a'looking at everything like it pleased him to be back. Well, ye knowed Vince. He han't one to talk much, but the boys told me what happened. Poor old man. He axed Vince did he recollect him, and he said yeah, he had never fergit him. Then Reece axed could he come and live with us, said how he would give him his hoss and what money he had if he would take him in and keep him long as he had to live."

Cindy took the corner of her apron and wiped her eyes, and then went on. "Vince never even stopped working, jest said, 'Paw, ye never cared what happened to me and my brothers and sisters. When we was little ye left maw and went off. Now ye come to me. I don't want ye hoss nor ye money, and I don't want you.' That's what the boys told me."

"Well, I lay waid him as he come back out of the holler. He looked so pitifullike. I tried to git him to come in and eat a bite, but he wouldn'. I took him out a plateful of grub and some coffee. I know he treated his wife and family real mean, goin' off that way. But I still felt sorry fer him. Vince told him to go stay with his Indian young'uns. Well, anyway, I hate to go agin Vince. It sure is good to talk about it."

"Well, let's don't fergit the cabbage plants," Frankie said. "I hope they han't took the hard shanks a'staying here too long."

"They look alright to me," Cindy answered as she stooped to pull up the cabbage plants.

Frankie broke several large leaves from a "pie plant" nearby, and as Cindy pulled the plants up and handed them to her friend, Frankie rolled the rhubarb leaves around their roots. Each woman was in deep thought.

"Well, ye better go home with me. Guess I'll take this short cut through ye truck patch."

"Ye jest better stay all day," Frankie returned.

When the older woman entered her door she heard Kitteneye laughing.

"Well, what's ticklin' ye so. Ye are smiling like a summer possum."

"Why, Maw," Kitteneye said, "Cindy done and went off and fergit her baby."

"I do declare." She ran to the door and looked up the road. "Maybe I can holler to her 'fore she gits too fer. Oh, no, she is clear out of sight. Well!"

"Maw, can we git to keep her?" the boy asked.

"Well, ye know she'll recollect her 'fore she gets much

further. She was a'worrin' a'right smart. But to fergit ye own newborn baby. I never heard of such. She will sure be plagued when she comes back."

"Yeah, bet her face will be as red as her hair," laughed Kitteneye. "Oh, Maw, can I nuss the baby 'fore she comes back?" he pleaded.

"Yeah, don't see how it would hurt anything. Ye beat everything I ever seed, the way ye take to young'uns, ye being a boy child."

Frankie went to the bed and brought the baby to where Kitteneye sat in his chair.

"Now hold ye hand to its back and don't tetch the soft place there in the top of its head. Ye can kill a young'un by mashing that soft spot."

They both looked up as they heard the gate open and Cindy soon burst through the door.

"Say, did ye ever hear tell of such a person goin' off and fergitten their own flesh and blood baby?" She dropped on the nearest chair and began to fan her face with her bonnet.

"Kitteneye was a'hopin' ye wouldn't come back a'tall. He wants to keep her," Frankie explained.

After a few more moments of talking Cindy took her baby and again started for the door.

"Ye all go up with me," she said.

Kitteneye said, "Ye can take her now but someday I'll come git her."

"All right, son," Cindy promised, "some day I'll give her to ye when she is all growed up, puny as you are. If'n she takes after the Owens, she will catch up with you."

They both knew they were speaking in jest. Little did they know that these words would be remembered for many a day, repeated several times, and even told for generations to come.

For this was the first time my father met my mother, Sarah, his future wife.

You have also found out how we became known as the Summer Slones, a nickname that everyone in Knott County (who can lay claim to it), wears proudly, even to the fifth and sixth generations.

CHAPTER FOUR

MY GRANDMA FRANKIE made "tied lace," a handcraft that is now a lost art. At least, no one in our family knows how to make it, though I have seen a few pieces. My stepmother had some sheets that were edged with "hand-tied lace." I remember it was a heavy, thick lace and must have been made from twine. She used no needle and simply made it by tying the threads together by hand. It was very beautiful. She used many different patterns: She made small edging for sheets, pillowcases, and underclothing for the women; and she also made a large curtain. Folks hung these from a pole just under the ceiling, in one of the back corners of the house. Behind it all their "wearing things" were hidden from view. They could also have a little privacy to bathe or change clothes by getting behind this curtain.

Grandma made the tied lace to sell at the small towns. She would work at these all winter. Then in the spring she would go and swap them for salt, coffee, and the very few things that her family had to have and could not raise or make themselves.

One morning in the early spring of 1874, way before daybreak, Frankie and Kitteneye started for Walker Town. They had a load of these spreads and some dried roots. They wanted to get an early start for they had a long walk before them. "Now it's sure chilly this morning," the small boy said.

"Yeah, but it'll be hot agin the sun gits up. Not backing out on me are ye son?"

"No, I am much pleased to go. And Maw, you did say you might git us some brown sugar?"

"Yeah, I shore will. Say, I tell you what us do, jest wrap these spreads 'round our head and shoulders. They will keep us warm. Be careful and don't let 'em hang down and get wet. They'll be ruint if'n ye do."

So up the road they went. Soon Frankie, who was in front, stopped and whispered, "Be quiet. I reckon I hear a mule comin'." Although it was still quite a while before daylight, these mountain travelers knew this road like the back of their hand and did not need much light. But the mule meant someone was coming, and if they did not get out of the narrow path that ran along side of the creek, the precious white spread would get splattered with mud when the mule and rider passed.

So they climbed up on the side of the hill, just out of the road, but back under the trees in the semidarkness. Frankie placed her hand on her small son's shoulder, and he knew she wanted him to be quiet, until they saw who else was out as early as they were.

Just as soon as the mule turned the bend in the road and came in full view, Kitteneye saw it was his Grandfather Billie. But when Billie saw them he gave a gasp and groan, "Oh, my God, I am seeing a haunt, two haunts."

Frankie dug her fingers into Kitteneye's back hard and said shush to him, as Billie raised his trembling hand up before his face and made a cross in the air.

"The Father, The Son, and The Holy Ghost, what do ye want with me?" he moaned.

Then in a deep, throaty voice Frankie said, "Your son Jim is sick and in bed, and has no meat for him or his young'un, while you have a'plenty. Go back home and git two of ye biggest middlins and a ham. Take them to him, or if ye don't I will haunt ye all ye born days."

Billie did not wait to hear anymore, but turned his mule and rode back home.

Frankie and Kitteneye could hardly wait until he got out of hearing distance to begin laughing.

"Don't never mention this to a livin' soul," Frankie finally said when she caught her breath.

"But, Maw, I don't see how you thought so fast."

"Well, maybe we are haunts," she laughed.

Next evening when they returned home, Jim met them at the door with the news that his father had brought two large middlins (sides of salt bacon) and one smoked ham. Jim could not understand why.

"Didn't he tell ye any reason fer givin' ye this meat? He han't much fer givin' ye anything. Allus has been tight as the bark on a tree." Frankie could hardly keep from laughing.

"Nah, 'spect it was 'cause I am his son and he is my father."

Kitteneye looked at his mother and whispered, "Yeah, the father, the son, and the holy haunts."

CHAPTER FIVE

MY FATHER WAS not the only man on Caney to have a nickname, and he had more than one. He was also called Tow Wad. Tow was the thread left over from making cloth from hemp or cotton. A small wad of this tow was used to load their old "hawg rifflers." My father, being so small, was called Tow Wad. He was also called Lick Skillet, for the same reason. He said all the other boys ate the grub and he had to lick the skillet where it had been cooked.

Our mountain people love to "name after each other." It is a great honor to have the same name as an uncle, aunt, or grandfather. I even know several folks named for their own sister or brother. It did get kind of confusing to try and keep it straight, especially when we all lived so close together. So nicknames were a "must do," or necessity. Four of the first white people to live on Caney—Alice, Isom, Isaac, and Shady—have many namesakes. You will find these names in almost all the Slone families. At one time there were eleven Isom Slones on Caney: my father Kitteneye, Fat

Isom, Big Isom, Pot Stick, Stiller, Hard's Isom, Andy's Isom, Jailor Isom, Preacher Isom, Crazy Isom, and Salty Ice. Sometimes the father's name was added on, so as to tell just which one you were referring to, like Hard's Isom and Andy's Isom. Often using the father and grandfather's name, for example, we said, Hard's Billie's Pearce, though I could never understand why as he was the only man named Pearce that I ever knew. Of course the women had nicknames too, as they were also named after someone else. When a boy was named for his father, it would be Big Sam and Little Sam. This begins to get funny when Little Sam weighs over 200 pounds and is six feet tall. My husband is still called Little Willie by some folks, although his Uncle Willie has been dead for over fifty years.

Sometimes the last names were nicknamed. There were so many Slones that we had to have nicknames for the different families. Of course we are all Kitteneyes. Grandpa Jim's were the Summer Slones, my husband's folks were the Jim Bows.

Almost everyone enjoyed their nicknames, although there were some who got angry if you called them that to their face. I know one man who killed his nephew over a nickname. I was an eyewitness to this, and I will tell it as I remember, changing very little except the names.

Hank, the nephew, was an orphan. His father had been killed in a shooting accident just a few months after his mother had died. He and his youngest sister stayed with their grandparents; his twin brothers, who were about five or six, stayed with Uncle Josh. I don't think Josh was very good to the twins. I know of one time when my father stopped him from giving them a whipping, but then father would not let anyone whip a child. He said there "was not a place on a child big enough to hit." So there might have been "hard feeling" between Hank and his Uncle Josh, even before the nickname began. Josh had gotten burned in the face when he was a child. The burn had not been deep enough to leave a scar, but it did cause no beard to grow on almost all his chin. There was a very small patch on one side. For this reason someone called him Nine Beard. When Hank found out that it upset his uncle to be called this, he would call him that all the more. The more Hank said it, the madder Josh got. Soon all the kids began yelling at him every time they passed his house or met him in the road. They would sing, "Nine Beard, Nine Beard, split one, make ten."

My father's house was next door to Josh's. In the night sometimes we would hear Hank and his friends yelling as they passed, "Nine Beard, Nine Beard, split one, make ten." We would hear Josh yelling back insults. My father tried to talk to him. He would say, "Don't let them know it bothers you and they will hush." But Josh would only say, "I'll hush 'em if I have to kill 'em."

One night a lot of us young folks had been to the Community Center, for a play or show—something to which all the Creek children had been invited. After it was over we had gathered in the post office, all laughing and having a good time. I saw Josh stick his head in the door of the post office. He looked like a wild man. I did not see a gun in his hand, but some of the other kids said later that they did. He just looked over the crowd and left "without saying a word." Somehow we none felt like fun any more so we started home. One of Josh's daughters and I were the last to leave. I had kind of wanted to wait until father came in with the mail and walk home with him, but the other girl seemed frightened and asked me to go with her. There were perhaps twenty, more or less, of us—all grouped off in twos and threes. My own young nephew was just ahead of us; he was holding on to Hank's hand. I heard Hank begin "Nine

Beard, Nine Beard." I remember thinking, "Oh, no, not tonight." And then I heard the gunfire. It was only then that I noticed Josh. Hank stumbled, staggered, and started running across the creek and into Manis Slone's house as the gun kept blasting. Everyone began screaming. That has been almost fifty years ago, but I still recall it all. For awhile I was so stunned I could not move; I did not even think to see about my small nephew, but began running back toward the post office. I must get to my father (as always I thought he could make everything alright again). He had just left the post office. I ran into his arms and sobbed, "Papa, Josh has killed Hank."

"Are ye shore?"

"Yes, I saw it. I saw the bullet hit him. I saw his shirt jump."

"Where is he?" my father asked, and I told him that I saw him run into Manis Slone's house. "Well, if he can still walk, then maybe he is not dead. Let's go see. Don't tell anyone what you saw. There was plenty of other witnesses. I know what lawyers can do to a witness, and if you are really needed you can be used later."

When we got to Manis' house a large crowd had gathered; everyone was talking in whispers. I stayed in the yard and did not go in. After my father looked at Hank he said, "Hank, can you hear me?" He answered, "Yeah, Kitteneye, I can." Father said, "Hank, have you made peace with God?" And he answered, "Yeah, I know I am dying; tell Uncle Josh I forgive him." Hank lived only a few more hours. Father prepared Hank's body for burial, then went home. Josh "gave himself up to the law." He was tried and pronounced insane and sentenced to the prison for the criminal insane, where he died a few months later.

I did not have to be a witness, but my little nephew was, and he won the hearts of the whole courtroom. Because he was so young he was not allowed to be "sworn in." The judge took him upon his lap and talked to him.

"Well, Hal," the judge began after asking him his name and where he lived, "How old are you?"

"Six, might nigh seven."

"Do you know the difference between a lie and the truth?"

"Shore, Grandpa Kitteneye learned me that."

"What would happen to you if you told a lie?"

"Why, Grandpa would be awful plagued and mad to me."

"Would he whip you?"

"No, he never whup any'un."

"If you are not afraid of him, then why do you obey him?"

"Because I love him."

"Did he tell you what to say here today?"

"Just to tell the truth, like allus."

"You and Hank have the same last name. Are you kinfolks?"

"If we are, Grandpa never did learned me that."

"Was Hank your friend?"

"Sure, Hank was a friend to everyone."

"How long have you known Josh?"

"Why, a long, long time," Hal answered, "ever since I was a little boy."

You couldn't hear the judge's next question for all the laughter.

CHAPTER SIX

I KNOW THAT my father carried the mail when he was only seventeen. He was chosen by his parents to be the mailboy because his other brothers were larger and more able to do the heavy work. Also, because he was small, he was a less load for the mule to carry, not that there was ever much mail. Sometimes there were only a few letters in the "mail pockets."

He made only one trip each week, going somewhere near Harlan. He started out early Monday morning, getting to the end of his route on Wednesday evening. Then on Thursday, the journey home would begin. Sunday was spent at home. He must have spent the night with folks along the way, sleeping on the floor or sharing the bed with some of the menfolks. The mail pockets he had to keep with him always. That was his sworn duty. He would place them under his feet when he ate, even at the table, and under his head at night. It wasn't that he did not trust the people he came in contact with—this was a requirement by the government. And before you could become a mail boy there was a swearing-in ceremony. One of the things you promised to do was keep the mail bag that contained the first class mail with you at all times.

A mountain boy might not respect the laws of his government and even have contempt for anyone who enforced them, but his word was his honor. That he would not go back on. To call someone a liar to his face was putting your life in danger. So when Kitteneye "took an oath" to keep the mail with him at all times, that was just what he did.

He had many stories about his first job as a mail boy. One night a very bad storm came up all at once and he had to spend the night under a cliff. This cave had two separate rooms, divided by a large rock, which probably had been part of the roof at one time. But it looked safe enough and having no other choice, he and his horse were soon bedded down. He slept sound. He remembered waking up a few times during the night and hearing someone snore, but did not get aroused enough to pay attention to it. He slept very late the next morning and when he looked under the other side of the cliff, he found some footprints that told him he had spent the night with a bear.

Another time Kitteneye was delayed for some reason and had to find shelter with an old couple, who shared their only food with him, green onions. They had only one bed, so he slept stretched out before the fire. Next morning after chopping them some wood and piling it in the corner of the cabin, he continued his journey. He often worried how these old folks made out that winter, or if spring found them still alive.

He often carried his lunch—a piece of corn bread and saltback. He said he never knew how this grub could take up such a small place in his pocket and fill up such a big hole in his belly.

And once when his mule broke though the ice he almost

drowned trying to save the mail. Some way he managed to get out of the water and onto the mule's back. He did not remember anything else until he woke up in bed at the post master's house several miles away. He had not been able to call out when he arrived before the door and just by chance did they find him. His feet were frozen to the stirrups and and they had to "prize" his fingers loose from the mail pockets.

The winters were much colder back then. Sometimes the creeks would stay frozen over for weeks at a time. Then the mule would have to have "ice nails" in his shoes.

One such cold spell caught a snake in the middle of the stream as he was crossing from one side of the creek to the other. There he stayed, frozen stiff for many days. It happened to be close to the trail that Papa and his trusty mule, John Barney, were ambling along. As the long hours spent in the saddle were lonesome, looking for this frozen snake each time he passed became a pasttime and a small break in the monotony. He wondered what would happen when the water thawed.

As luck would have it, he chanced to be there when Mr. Snake finally was released from his prison and slowly but surely climbed the bank. Kitteneye saw, understood, and remembered.

Grandchildren, you get your education one way and he got his another.

CHAPTER SEVEN

KITTENEYE COULD TELL it was going to be a very beautiful day. He had been awaken by a crunching sound from the kitchen and a flopping beat, beat, which came from the direction of the fireplace. Both told him that breakfast was on the way. Maw was grinding coffee, and one of the girls was churning. He thought how good that fresh butter would taste with the molasses. He sure was hungry. He remembered he had not eaten a "plum mess" since breakfast the morning before. That nickel's worth of brown sugar and round crackers he had bought at the grocery store could hardly be called a snack. He had eaten them on his way back home.

He knew that Maw had left his supper for him on the table covered over with a cloth. He could have eaten, but he did not want to risk waking her up. He knew she would ask him why he had gone to town. He knew she would have to know sometime, but knowing how she would fret, he wanted to wait as long as he could.

He glanced over in the other beds. No one except Maw and the girls were up. He would wait until everyone else was getting up and maybe Maw would forget to question him in the confusion and noise. With some putting on their clothes, some at the washbench dousing their faces in the cold water, others using the comb, he might get by.

Soon they were all settled around the long table. Along the side next to the wall was a long bench. Here sat all the young ones side by side like crows on a fence. Chairs had been drawn up against the other side and here sat all the "big children and grown-ups." Paw was at one end near the bread. He would be the one to pass the bread. No mountain man would break bread from a woman's hand. The Good Book spoke against that. Maw was at the other end, near the stove, where she could reach the coffee pot, when someone wanted a second cup, or the one that needed to be "hit up" if it became cold.

There was a large square of corn bread, from which each person broke a chunk. Paw would break a piece and hand it to the ones who could not reach it themselves. A big platter of fried meat swimming in its own grease, a bowl of gravy, some fried potatoes. The fresh butter and the ever-present jug of molasses—maybe not so fancy but very nourishing.

Kitteneye finished his breakfast real fast, then, pushing his chair from the table, he hurried for the door.

"Wait, son, I want to talk to you," Frankie said.

"I am in sort of a hurry. Be back in a minute," he answered. He sure did not want her to ask him now, for he had never told her a lie in his life and he did not want to talk before the whole family.

As he went toward the barn, he thought, "I will just go on now." He was still wearing his best clothes and the piece of paper was in his pocket. So he caught his mule and put the saddle on it. No one had come outside. He turned the mule and started up the road.

When he got to Vince Owens' house he stopped and got off his mule, tied the bridle to a fence post, and went in.

He knocked at the door and a voice from within told him to "Come in, if your nose is clean." He pushed the door open. Sarah and her mother were sitting before the fireplace. The young girl's lap was full of wool, with a full basket by her side. They were carding the wool, which would later be spun into yarn.

When Sarah saw who had entered the room, she put her hand up to her mouth, then dumping all the wool into the basket, she got up and made a fast retreat for the kitchen.

"Well, well," laughed Cindy, "you sure have plagued Sarah. She thought it was one of the young'uns a'foolin' us. She never dreamt it was someone a'comin' in. She would never a'said that to you. Well, git ye a chair and sit a spell," she finished. Kitteneye sat down in the chair, now vacated by Sarah.

"Where is ye old man, Cindy?" he asked. He did not really want to know, but good manners demanded that he ask.

"He took a turn of corn to the mill," she answered, still working away with her wool and wooden cards.

"Yeah, I fergit it was mill day."

"Isom," she asked in a very concerned voice, "what fer are ye all dressed up in your Sunday go to meetin' clothes and it be a weekday?"

"Well," he said, "that's why I stopped. I wanted to tell ye I am git'n married today."

"Kitteneye, are ye goin' to marry Jane Hughes?" she exclaimed.

"Yeah, I went to town and got my license yesterday. I am on my way to her house now."

"But son, do you like her a whole lot?" she asked. They had always been real good friends and Cindy knew she could speak freely with him.

"Well," he mused, "I 'spect it is more for Cleveland's sake, and I am twenty-four years old. Most everybody else has been married a long time, agin they are that old. You know she lays Cleveland to me," he blushed when he said this.

"Yeah, I jest about know he is your'n. If ever a child daddied itself, he shore does. He is jest the spittin' image of ye. But I shore hate to see ye marry her."

They sat there for a while, both lost in their own thoughts. Finally, Cindy began to laugh.

"Anyway, I thought I had been raisin' ye a good girl. I have teased Sarah about you and told her how that I fergit her that time, and went off and left her at ye maw's house. You shore had made ye mind up to keep her then."

"Well, it's not altogether been a joke with me, but I just got mixed up with Jane, and anyway there's Cleveland. Sarah would not want to be bothered with him."

"Well, Kitteneye, I told ye I was raisin' ye a good girl. If ye want to wait a few more months, I believe everything will work itself out. Lay them license there in the fire."

"Alright," he said, and taking the paper from his pocket, he slowly placed it in the fire and watched as it curled, then caught, and soon became ashes.

"A long trip to town and two dollars all went for nothin'," he laughed. "but less ways I won't haf'n to tell Maw after all."

Then he turned to Cindy and said, "Well, ye are willin', the preacher is, and I am. I guess I will just have to talk Sarah into being willin'."

Sarah, who had been eavesdropping during all this talk, whispered to herself, "That's not goin' to be as hard a job as you suspect, Kitteneye."

And it must not have been too much trouble. In the year 1887, and on the twenty-eighth day of July, John L. Slone, an Old Regular Baptist minister, pronounced them man and wife. And they loved each other until they were separated by death.

CHAPTER EIGHT

I DON'T KNOW very much about their courtship days, but I don't think my story would be complete unless I told you of one happening that almost brought an end to their friendship before it had barely begun. They were planning on going to church that day, around on Hollybush. Sarah was to wait before the house, near the "chop block," while Kitteneye went to catch his mule. So while Sarah stood there in all her best clothes and a with a blanket folded to use as a cushion, Kitteneye took the bridle and started for the pasture.

He soon located Old Barney. But a large patch of ragweed, now in bloom, stood between him and the mule. He took one look at those weeds and then thought what they would do to his nice new britches. His mother had sewn them from cloth she had woven herself. She had even raised the flax and spun the thread. She had not dyed the cloth, so they were a kind of cream color, almost white. Those weeds were damp with dew and loaded with yellow pollen. If he walked through there, his pants would be ruined.

He glanced back over his shoulder and saw he was well out of sight. Pulling his pants off, he hung them on the pasture fence and went after the mule in his shirttail.

The mule did not want to be caught. He had found some very nice tasty grass and he preferred eating to going to church. It took Kitteneye quite a while, but he finally won out and put the bridle where it belonged, on Old Barney, and led him back to the fence where he had left his britches.

He looked and looked. He knew this was the right place, where he had climbed over the fence. He could still see the path of trampled-down weeds. What he could not see was his britches.

Then, he glanced over on the other side of the pasture fence, and lo and behold, there stood a two-year-old steer a'chomping away at his new pants while he stood there in his shirttail.

He rescued what was left, which was very little, not even enough to wear.

"Now what a mess I've got myself in," he said to himself. "Devil take that old calf."

The only way out of the hollow was right past the house, where Sarah was waiting. He hoped she had given up and gone inside. There was only one thing to do.

He mounted his mule, and started him running at a very fast lope. He did not even glance at the house. He saw Sarah through the corner of his eye, as the astonished mule went flying by with Kitteneye on its back, without saddle or pants.

I don't know how he ever explained it to her, but I guess they had many a good laugh about the time they did not go to church together.

CHAPTER NINE

I DON'T KNOW if they had a "workin'" when there was a log cabin to be built for my parent's first home. If so, all their brothers decided on a given day. Everyone on Caney was invited or asked to come. Bringing their own tools, they built a one-room cabin, to which more could be added later. The trees had been cut and hauled to the site before by Kitteneye, with a pair of oxen.

Each man did what he was best at; some hewed, and some notched the ends of the logs. Then everyone helped to place them on top of each other. The ridgepole was the hardest one to get in place, and even the womenfolk sometimes helped when there weren't enough men present. The roof was made of split boards, with the space between daubed with mud and clay taken from the creek banks. A chimney was built on the side, a door opening on another side. The door "shutter" was also made from split boards. Split logs were smoothed on the flat side to make the floor, and were called "puncheons." To keep these floors clean, they were scrubbed with beat-up sand rocks and a scrub broom.

I guess Kitteneye built his own chimney. I know he was a good hand to build chimneys. They used slate rocks, which were easier to chip and form. Stuck together with clay, they were not so heavy to stack. There would be a large open fireplace for heating and cooking. A large "back log" big enough to burn for several days was placed in the back of the fireplace, and a "fore log" placed in front, each end laying on a rock, or on a block of iron. This was so the fire could get air. Smaller pieces of wood were stacked crisscross so they would catch fire easy. The kindling would be put under this and lighted with a spark, made by beating a piece of steel against a flint stone. Many times when the fire had gone out, one of the kids would be sent to a neighbor to borrow some burning pieces of wood. So if someone seems to be in a hurry, we use the expression, "What did you come for? A shevilful of fire?"

At the working the women would be busy cooking a good dinner: chicken and dumplings for sure, plenty of fried eggs, meat either cooked or fried, large stacks of gingerbread and sweetcakes, egg custards, apple pie, maybe shucking beans or corn field peas, blackberry dumplings, and pots and pots of coffee.

These folks worked hard and ate hearty. There was always plenty to eat. If it was summertime, someone's job was to keep the flies from getting on the table. This was accomplished by waving a small branch or twig broken from a tree, backwards and forwards, over the food, while everyone was eating. Someone else took her place with the "swithin'" while she ate.

The men were fed first, then the women and children, but there was always enough for everyone and a lot of jokes and plenty of laughter. They worked together, ate together, and loved each other as neighbors were intended to do since time began. I think a lot was lost when these old ways were changed to so-called better ones.

I am not going to say that everyone got along together in love and fellowship. There were quarrels and disputes, even ending in fights and gun battles. Some men were killed. That has been told and written about, but I hope to show you another life, one that was more real and true: people who joined together to help their neighbors. A working was a social event that was enjoyed by everyone. A lot of work was done, a lot of food eaten, and a lot of enjoyment had by all.

Some folks had a dance the night after the working, but I am almost sure Kitteneye and Sarah did not. Both Sarah and Kitteneye's parents were Old Regular Baptists, and music and dancing are not allowed by our church.

I guess there would have been some drinking of "good corn liquor." Drinking moonshine, so long as you did not get drunk, wasn't thought of as a sin back then. I have been told that even the preachers would take a drink now and then. My stepmother said her parents always kept a large barrel of moonshine sitting inside their cabin door, with a cup on a nail above, so anyone, even the small children, could take some whenever they desired. Moonshine whiskey was used a lot for medicine.

I do not know if Sarah's first home was built by friends and neighbors, or by Kitteneye himself. I don't even know just where it was. I do know it was somewhere on the head of Caney Creek, near Trace. He once told me how he made their first bed out of poles stuck into the cabin logs, in one corner. Then he laced the poles together with strips of leather for springs. The mattress was a cloth bag filled with shucks, and I am almost sure my grandmother gave them a feather bed and pillows. All mountain girls had a supply of quilts made by the time they were old enough to get married, beautiful quilts, an art in their designs and with stitches so small you had to look close to see them, patterns such as Double Wedding Ring, Robbin' Peter To Pay Paul, Drunkards' Path, and many, many others. These patterns were exchanged with neighbors and friends and were regarded as very precious.

In a like way, mountain people would help each other butcher their hogs. Even the small kids and women would do what they could. From the beginning, when the fire was built to heat the water, until the hairs were cleaned up and burned, much work had to be done. The chickens must not eat the hairs. If they did, they would take the "squalks" and die.

There was a lot of fun. Someone would be asked to measure the hog's tail. If he had never heard the joke before, he would be told to place his finger along the underside of the hog's tail to see how far it would reach up his arm. Then with a quick push the poor unsuspecting guy's finger would end up in the hole under the hog's tail. As the now wiser embarrassed fellow went to wash his hands, everyone would laugh. This was childish and simple, but it made life more enjoyable and changed what would have been hard work into play.

As soon as the liver was removed from the hog, great chunks were thrown on the fire to "brile." These the children would eat just as soon as they were cooked enough to be edible.

The bladder was saved and made into a balloon. Even the intestines or "guts" were used. They were cleaned, washed, and dried to be later made into soap.

The small pieces and scraps left over from rendering the lard were called "cracklin's." These were used to make soap. They were also very good mixed with cornmeal and water, to make "cracklin' bread."

My father always said that all of the hog was used except the "squeal," and if he could find a use for it, he would try to save that. Anyway his children squealed enough to suit him.

A large kettle of the meat was cooked and after everyone

had eaten, each neighbor was given a "mess" to take home. The rest was "salted down" or made into sausage.

It's better not to feed your hogs just before killing them, since they are easier to clean and the feed is not wasted. But my father always fed his. He said he did not want anything to die hungry.

Another happy time was a "molassie stir-off." Every family had a crop of cane that had to be harvested just as soon as the seeds became ripe. If left standing any longer, the stalks began to dry. If cut too soon, the molasses would have a sour taste and would not keep. There was usually just one person in a community with a gin mill and a molasses pan. Kitteneye owned one.

He would take his equipment, set it up near the crop of cane, and begin his work. All the neighbors would gather to help. The seed pods were saved for chicken feed. The blades were dried for fodder. The stocks were cut and run through the gin mill. The juice was then boiled in the large pan placed over a fire.

When it first begins to boil, a green slimy scum is formed on top. This must be dipped off with a long-handled skimmer. This scum was thrown into a large hole dug in the ground. It was always a big joke if someone slipped and fell into this messy hole. They would use any trick to get each other into this hole.

When the molasses had boiled enough, a plug was pulled from a hole in one corner of the pan. The fragrant foamy liquid was caught in barrels or empty lard cans.

Eating molasses foam is one of my most pleasant childhood memories. We would take a stalk of cane and dip into the molasses, twirling it around until it was covered with a thick layer, licking it off while it was still hot. Everyone ate from the pan or barrel; maybe not so sanitary, but real enjoyment—better than marshmallow.

My father received some of the molasses in payment for his work and the use of his gin and pan. Every visitor was given a bucket or jarful, to take home.

One of my cousins told me that he found a barrel of molasses on his porch one morning. He knew it had been left there by Uncle Kitteneye. He and his brothers and sisters were very pleased with this gift. Their father at that time was being detained against his own will at the government's expense at Frankfort. He had been caught in the wrong place at the wrong time by the wrong people.

My father also made chairs. I don't know when he first began or who he learned this trade from, so he may have made the first ones to have been used by Sarah in her new home.

As I have said, these folks thought nothing of working twelve hours a day. Kitteneye told me that one day after they had worked all day hoeing the corn, he and my mother came home at the edge of dark, very tired. While she prepared their supper, he sat down in the door and laid back on the floor to rest. When she got her bread in the dutch oven and placed it before the fire, she also came and sat down in the door and stretched out beside him. They soon fell asleep and were awakened the next morning when their cow decided it was milk time and stuck her head in the door and gave a loud moo.

I wish I knew a lot more about their life together. I know they worked hard. As for "book learnin'," my mother knew only one letter, the letter "O." But she was educated in the things she needed to know: how to raise a family; how to card wood, and spin it to yarn; how to dye the yarn with bark and roots gathered from the hillside, which of these to use to get the color she wanted; and how to knit this yarn into stockings and caps for her husband and children. With some help, she sheared wool from her own sheep.

She knew when to plant her garden, which plants grow better in one soil than another, when to fertilize—using manure from the barn and chicken house, and rotten cinders and ashes from the fireplace—and how much was needed.

She loved to make her rows of beans and peas as straight as an arrow, dragging up large "ridges" or beds for her sweet potatoes, beets, and parsnips. She had artistic interest in how pretty she could make them look. She knew how to grow all the different vegetables, when to plant, to hoe, and gather them. She knew how to dry the green beans, to make shuck beans, and how to dry the "punkin" and cushaw (crookneck squash) for winter use. She sliced them into rings, about an inch wide, and hung them from a pole over the fireplace. She would have large barrels of shelled beans for soup beans. She knew how to make sauerkraut and pickled corn and beans.

She had a very large garden—row after row of vegetables—but the very best, with the richest soil, she used for her flowers: fall roses (zinnias), marigolds, bachelor's buttons, and touch-me-nots, and many others, too many to name.

My mother had no education, but in the things she needed to know, she had a master's degree, given to her by the greatest Master of them all. She knew the value of prayer, and how to serve the Lord. She joined the Old Regular Baptist Church when she was very young. In fact, she was one of the first eight to form the Mt. Olive Church.

She never went further away from home than five miles in her whole life. She had gone to the Lower Caney Church house and had crossed the hills to the Reynolds Fork Church and Carr's Church. She had even gone to visit her daughter that lived in Mallet. But she had never gone to see her oldest daughter living in Ball, no more than twenty miles away.

I know she had rambled all over these hillsides as a child

and young woman, hunting her cow and sheep, and bringing them in from the pastures. She had gone to dig roots, and gather barks and leaves, to make her dye and medicine, picking berries and gathering stovewood. I am almost sure she also went with my father to "fight fire," when the woods would get on fire and all the neighbors would join together. There were two ways a fire was "let out." First, every spring the "sage" grass was burned off the pastures to give way for the new grass to come up. Second, when a new ground was cleared, meaning all the trees cut down, the large logs were hauled away for use as firewood or buildings, and the smaller limbs were then piled up and burned. We called it burning brush. This was a get-together for all the neighbors, but sometimes the fire got out of control. The greatest danger was to the split rail fence. Many times Sarah and Kitteneye would pitch all the rails down the hill in advance of an oncoming fire to save them, later going back and carrying them, one at a time, to rebuild the fence.

My mother loved to cook, and fed everyone who came to her door. If anyone passed the house near mealtime, she would ask them to come in and eat with her. She often said she hoped no one had passed her house hungry.

They had a large family, so the table was extra long. My mother always had this big long table filled with bowls and platters of food, more than enough for her own family.

My sister told me of one time when seven men stopped in out of a rain storm. They were on their way from Carr, going to Wayland to work in the coal mines. When the men came into the house, my mother had dinner on the table. She asked the men to eat with them. All she added extra on the table were the seven plates and seven knives and forks. Yet everyone had all they wanted to eat.

The mountain folks took the words in the marriage

ceremony, "What God has joined together let no man put asunder," for what they were meant to be. No man talked very much to another man's wife unless the husband was present. On entering the house for a visit, he asked at the door where the "old man" was. If he wasn't at home, he would not come in. If the man of the house was working somewhere near, he would go find him. If the job was something at which he could help, he would do so, while talking.

If it was cold weather and there were some of the "big young'uns" at home, the visitor might stay for a little while, even if the husband was gone. The woman would always ask about the other's wife, and ask him to bring her and come see them sometimes.

When two mountain people met, they always asked each other to go home with them, and when anyone passed the house he was asked to come in. The one who was passing also asked the other folks to go home with him. This was a very strict code of the hills, and it was very bad manners if you did not observe them. Another rule is to always follow a visitor who is leaving to the door and talk with him until he is outside and always ask him to come back soon.

If a woman or man was said to be "clever," that meant they were unselfish and anyone was welcome to eat with them. If a woman or a girl was called "honest," it did not mean she would not steal, but that she had high moral values. Of course, there were a few "mean" women or "ridge runners" who were free with their favors, and gave themselves to any man who asked. These women were always shunned by all the "honest" women. A bastard or "wool colt" was fed and clothed, but never fully accepted. I remember being scolded by my father because I walked up the road one evening after school with a boy who did not know who his father was. This was a "double standard," for father had two children of his own without being married to their mother. As this is a true story, I must tell the bad as well as the good. My half-brothers were a part of our family, as much as anyone. The oldest one, Cleveland, is now buried in our family graveyard.

We people of the mountains are very clannish, with a family unity and closeness hard to understand and still harder to explain. You cannot help but notice how the same name will appear on mailboxes and business fronts: a few miles through the mountains and there will be only Halls, then Collins, to be replaced by Gayhearts. From all the old folks who obtained grants to land you will still find some bearing the same name, living on the same land. My own grandchildren are the tenth generation of Slones who were born, lived—and the first seven generations died and buried—here on Caney, within two miles of the same place where they settled in 1790.

CHAPTER TEN

My MOTHER WAS one of the very few on Caney who could not read and who had no learning at all. The eight grades were all that were taught. You could then go to Hindman, where George Clark had a teacher training class. If you completed this and could pass the exam given by the state, you were qualified to teach.

I know the eighth grade is far from a college education, but it can not be classed as illiterate. In reading, spelling, arithmetic, history and geography, the grades were more advanced than that which is taught in school now, though in science and arts, they knew very little. If you had completed the fifth grade under these old teachers, you would have known about the same as an eighth grader does now.

Much more than half of our Caney folks finished the grades before 1916, and many became teachers. My oldest sister, Flora Belle Fugate, was one of these teachers; her husband was also.

We also had some very good lawyers, not on Caney, but in

Knott County. My uncle ElCaney Slone was one. He had always been the sickly one of the family and so he got more education. Sickly as he was, he lived to be over 100 years old.

There were many people who had talents. Some made beautiful chairs and fern stands with a "handmade lay" turned by a foot-powered pedal. Charley Huff made beautiful baskets accurate to size, holding either a peck, half-bushel, or one bushel.

Sarah Reynolds and Martha Watson wove beautiful blankets. I remember my mother had some of these. I have a small coat made from a piece of this hand-woven cloth. They raised the sheep, processed the wool, even dyed it with a dye made from roots and bark. They had intricate patterns of checks and stripes.

When my mother died, her home contained many pieces of furniture made by Preacher Billie Slone, a shelf for dishes called a cupboard, and a writing desk with several small drawers, expertly made. He had decorated them by making a notched edge using only an auger and handsaw. I still have the quilt shelf he made for my mother in payment for two bushels of "shelled-out" beans.

Their love of beauty was shown in the many beautiful quilts. They raised the cotton to pad these, though I don't think they spun any cotton. They did grow hemp and spun a crude kind of linen that they called homespun cloth.

Their shoes were moccasins made from leather, skinned from a cow or mule that had died from old age or disease, or a cow killed for food. My father said he was grown before he owned a pair of store-made shoes. He worked three days hoeing corn at twenty-five cents a day for some old man who lived at Jone's Fork. The shoes cost seventy-five cents a pair and the brand name was "stronger than the law." These heavy, awkward shoes were made in the same style for men and women, and in sizes for children also.

Some children would go barefoot all winter, staying in the house all the time except for the few moments each day when the call from nature came. When this happened, a large smooth board was heated before the fire and carried along to supply a warm place for the feet. The board was taken back to the house to be used again next time.

My stepmother told of using a "hot board" to stand on when they were washing clothes, or working at the loom. She said they were so careful with their "stronger than law" store shoes that they carried them with them to church, stopping just outside the door of the meeting house to put their shoes on. Sometimes the boyfriend would have the pleasure of carrying a girl's shoes for her. They used sheep tallow for polish.

That they were artistic and loved beauty is shown in so many ways. Mountain people grew "corn beads" or "Job's tears." The seeds are very pretty, with a hole through the center, and can be strung like beads. They decorated beautiful "comb cases" and picture frames for the walls of their homes with these beads.

For wallpaper, they pasted up newspaper and magazines. I taught my children the alphabet from my walls. My kids also invented a kind of "hide-and-go-seek" game. One would describe a picture or repeat a sentence seen somewhere on the wall. The first one to discover it got to choose the next. Living in these magazine walls gave you a feeling of being inside a storybook.

I always tried to read everything in these papers before I "papered the house." If not, I would sometimes get so interested in something I saw I would stop to read, and my paste would all dry up.

Almost every housewife knew how to sew and made clothes for her family. I have a picture of a large group of men and women who lived on Caney. They are nicely dressed, in the styles that were popular at the time—somewhere near 1890. I am sure their clothes were "homemade." A few had sewing machines; most sewed by hand.

They were intelligent folks, skilled and educated well in what they needed to know, because they had to make do with what they had.

That was a lesson I grew up with. We threw away nothing. To us a patch was not a bright colored swatch, placed "haper-scaper" on our jeans to make them look fancy. We patched our clothes to prolong their life and to keep the wind from whistling through a hole. Sometimes we even patched the patches.

There was not much we could do to make our shoes last longer except "half-sole" them and replace the strings with a strip of groundhog hide. When the hole in the crown of a man's hat became so large that it would no longer stay on his head, the brim was cut into strips and used for lamp wicks.

When quilts had outgrown their usefulness for the beds, they made saddle blankets, covers for a chicken coop, a dog bed, or they were hung over the opening of the outhouse or barn in place of a door shutter, or placed on the floor as a pallet for the baby. Our dish rags and wash clothes were from worn-out wearing things. An old meal sack became a towel. No Pampers hung from tree limbs along the creek. We used old bed sheets—after they became so thin you could sun bees through them—for diapers or "diddies" as we called them. A tick, a large cloth bag filled with corn shucks, was a mattress. For folks that did not keep geese or ducks and did not kill enough chickens to get feathers for pillows, the seed pods from milk weed did just fine. A man's shaving brush was also made from shucks. The razor strap was a good "chastising rod." My father always said, "if used enough it makes children walk straighter."

Even our toys were "make do's." A few gravels placed in an empty tobacco can became a rattle for baby. Empty thread spools strung together were another plaything. Jackstones were small chunks from a broken churn or crock. I was in high school before I knew you were supposed to have a small ball to go with the game of Jackstones. There were many games to be played with corn: Fox and Geese, Five Up, Hully Gully. Toy animals were made from cornstalks and everyone knows about the corn shuck dolls. Corncobs were made into pipes and also burned as fuel.

A washtub could be kept from leaking for a while by sprinkling cornmeal in it. After burning tar paper over the hole, some people used homemade soap to plug up the leak. Put on wooden "runners," a tub became a sled to haul manure and cinders for the garden, or to haul off rocks. It could be a home for baby chicks to protect them from rats, or a feed trough for Old Bossie. It might be filled with dirt and planted with flower seeds. An old dish pan was often nailed to the roof, where the stove pipe came through, thus protecting the boards from the heat, and also keeping the rain from running down the pipe onto the stove. An old saw too dull to cut wood became "laid hoes" or "fire shevils." Did you know you could use a dead turtle's shell for a soap dish?

Empty lard buckets became lunch pails, water or milk containers, and when there was more company than plates to "go around," the younger children could "eat off" the bucket lids for plates. An empty cream can made an unbreakable cup for little children.

Ashes from the fireplace made a fine polisher for pots and pans and silverware. Sand was used to scrub our floors and wooden chairs.

We were always glad to get wooden boxes or crates, such as the ones packed with fruit. We nailed them to the walls for bookshelves, or for dishes or clothes.

Potatoes and apple peelings were saved and fed to the chickens or pigs. Sometimes if apples were "scarce," the hulls, or peelings, were cooked in water and the juice made into jelly. The rest was run through a sifter and became applebutter when mixed with sugar and spices.

Even the eggshells were not wasted. They were browned and fed to the hens, or strung on the twigs of a tree in the yard to become an "egg tree." All food not eaten by the family was fed to the farm animals. Once an "outsider" lady came to Caney to spend the summer. She rented a small house from my father. She asked him what she should do with her garbage. When told what we did with ours she bought a pig from him. That fall when she started home, she came to him and said, "I would like to sell the pig back to you. I have only used it for six months. I think I should get back at least half what I paid you for it. Don't you?"

CHAPTER ELEVEN

MY FATHER AND mother had a very large family. On October 9, 1914, she gave birth to her last child. Five weeks later she died.

She was never "out of bed" after I was born except once. My father had gone over "in the head of Hollybush" to bring sheep home. During the summer they were turned loose, as all stock were, to forage for themselves. There were no stock laws then. Everyone kept a fence around their crops and gardens. The animals ran loose. In the fall, they were rounded up and put in the barn lot or stall, where they could be fed and watered. As my father went past the house with the sheep, my mother came to the door to see them. This was the last time she ever walked.

Just a few nights before she died, she spoke to my father. He had pulled his bed up by the side of her bed so she could awaken him if she needed anything during the night. "Isom," she said, "Are you asleep?"

"Well, I was before ye spoke, but I am awake now. What do ye want?"

"I just want a talk. I wanta tell ye I han't goin' to get well."

"Now Sarah, don't talk like that. You're gettin' better every day."

"I've been showed I han't goin' to get well. I am kinda glad to go. I am so tired of bein' sick and I want to go home, and be with my little ones that have gone on to live with Jesus. I just hate to leave you and my children, especially this baby one. Will you promise me you will never have her whopped?"

Kitteneye could hardly speak for the tears, but he tried to talk jokingly.

"Ye know I never was one for whoppin' the young'uns. I allus left that up to you."

"I know, but I want you to promise you won't ever let anyone whop her."

And he answered, "I promise."

There were many times when this promise was to be remembered in the future. And this is why I never got a spanking in my life. Kitteneye would go to the teachers and tell them that if they could not teach me without spanking me to send me home. You would think that I would have been very naughty, but it worked the other way. I was afraid I would get sent home, so I was real good at school.

A few days after this talk, Sarah was feeling a lot better. The weather was warm for November. Elizabeth Slone had stopped in for a visit and to see "how Sarah was doing." Sarah had a piece of cloth from which she wanted some caps made for the baby. Little ones always wore caps, night and day, through the winter. Elizabeth had said she would be more than glad to sew the caps if Sarah could cut them out first.

Edna remembers that she was sitting, holding the baby on her lap. She was only seven years old herself. One of the older girls was looking for the piece of cloth.

Kitteneye had taken Frances with him to gather a sled of corn, just enough to feed on for a few days. He had been "putting off" gathering the whole crop until his wife got well enough to be left alone with just the girls. He had just got part of the way up the hollow when he heard someone ringing the dinner bell. He knew by the low mournful sound of that bell what had happened. He left his mule and sled and ran home just as fast as he could. But he was too late. His wife was dead. He always said he believed she recognized him standing at the foot of the bed, for she seemed to smile at him.

"She was jest a'sittin' there, laughin' and talkin' to us and all at once she put her hand up to her face and said, 'Oh, my head,'" Elizabeth told him.

In a daze, Kitteneye prepared his own wife for burial. This had to be done before the body became stiff. He placed her straight in the bed, tied her feet together, crossed her hands on her breast, and, using a cloth, he caught it under her chin and brought it up over her head and tied it. Two pieces of money were placed on her eyes, so the weight would keep them closed. This was a work of love; he would not have allowed anyone else to do this had there been anyone there. It was the last thing he could do for his wife, and a task he had performed for many a neighbor and friend.

Dora Bell Taylor bathed and dressed the body. Some of the children remembered that their mother had expressed a desire to be put away wearing her favorite black satin dress. Over this dress was put a white shroud made by Sarah Reynolds. Preacher Billie Slone made the coffin from seasoned wood, lined it with white cloth, and covered the outside with black cloth. The edges were trimmed with lace. Some folks used cotton to pad the inside bottom, but Sarah had a beautiful quilt she had made herself for this purpose.

Both the coffin and shroud were made in the home where the corpse lay.

We sent for all the children who were married. Flora Belle had married Sam Fugate and lived on Lower Ball. She had three children. Square Slone, one of our cousins, went after her. It took one day to make the trip there on a mule and another day to come back. Usually a body was only kept up one night after death, but Mother wasn't buried until the third day, because it took that long to get Flora word and bring her home.

Arminda said she remembers that another cousin, Isaac Slone, came to get her in Mallet. My mother had asked that the funeral be preached before she was buried, and not a year later as most folks then did. She did not want any drinking going on at her funeral, and she was afraid there would be, if it was delayed for a year.

This practice is still honored in some families. It probably began back in the days of the circuit rider preacher, who only came once a year in his round of visits.

Everything was done out of love and friendship: the grave was dug, the coffin made, the sewing done. None of these mountain friends thought of it as work and would have been insulted if anyone had offered them pay. To have paid for these services as we do today would have seemed to these folks like paying someone to kiss you.

When my mother was buried there was a small house built to cover the grave. These are now a forgotten part of the past. The lower part of the house was latticework and the roofs were made of rough board shingles. The tombstone was of slate rock with the name and dates crudely chipped in with handmade tools.

These houses protected the graves from the wild animals, and kept the rain from falling on a loved one's grave.

I remember my Grandmother and Grandfather Owens

had a larger house covering both their graves. It had a small door. Many times when my troubles and sorrows became too heavy for my childish heart, I would crawl through this door to cry in private. I always came away comforted.

These little gravehouses were torn down about 1940, very much against my wishes. The old board sign—whose words were burnt into the wood by using a hot poker—is gone from above the gate. It said, "God bless them that sleep here."

I guess my scribblings are like my crazy quilts, without any form or unity. The more I write, the more I remember. There are just so many things I want to say, maybe some are interesting only to me. Our young folks have lost so much without ever knowing they had it to lose.

CHAPTER TWELVE

O F ALL THE things my father taught me, I am thankful that I learned from him the enjoyment one could obtain from work. I did not know until I was grown that there were people who did not like to work, and not until my children were grown did I realize that some folks thought it was shameful to do manual labor. (I must admit, though, I do not like to do housework. I like for a house to be a home, a comfortable place to live, not a "show room.")

I wish I could pass on to my grandchildren how I feel about growing our own food. All good things come from God. But you seem so close to Him, one with nature, when you plant the tiny seeds, in faith that they will grow. Later there is the joy of gathering and storing away these results of your partnership with nature. The food you grow yourself tastes much better and seems a lot cleaner to me. It may not be "untouched by human hands," but at least you know whose hands they were.

Mike was once helping me to dig a mess of potatoes for

supper and asked, "Granny, why do you put your potatoes in the ground? Is it so your chickens can't get at them? Mother gets hers at the market."

I've always been thankful we owned a farm of our own, to grow corn, for example. A "new ground" (pronounced as one word) was best. This meant the ground had been cleared of all the trees and underbrush, and was now ready to be planted.

If you were lucky enough to have a new ground you would be assured of a good crop but a lot more work. It had to be all done by hand, using only hoes. Although most of the larger roots and stumps were removed—either by burning or dynamite, or sometimes pulled out by oxen—there were still too many small roots and sprouts to make plowing possible.

So, early in the spring, sometimes as early as January or February, we would begin "grubbin'," digging the young sprouts that were beginning to grow around where the trees had grown. After these were all dug, they were raked into piles and burned. Then we took hoes and shaved off the weeds. Each one working would take a "swith" and distance themselves as long as they could reach with a hoe, one above the other, each one just a little ahead of the one above. Around the hill they would go, raking a very small layer of the topsoil along with the weeds onto the row below. After this was finished, they would "dig in" the corn, about every three feet, in rows about four feet apart. A small loose hole was dug, with three to five grains of corn dropped inside, and the dirt spread over it. My father always said to plant five,

> One for the ground squirrel,
> One for the crow,
> One to rot,
> And two to grow.

When the corn was about a foot high, you began to hoe it, cutting all the weeds, and thinning it to two stalks to a hill. Someone would always joke and say, "Pull up the large ones and give the little ones room to grow." We replanted any missing hills and a few weeks later we hoed it again. This second hoeing was called "laying it by," because this finished all the work with the corn until time to save the fodder and gather the corn. The fodder was gathered in September and the corn brought to the barns in November. When we "layed by our corn" it called for a wild celebration. Folks on adjoining farms were always in friendly competition. Each would rush to beat the others. Our hills are so close, many different family groups could see and hear each other. When the last "hill of corn" was hoed they would begin to yell, beating their hoes together or against rocks, thumping on the dinner bucket, anything to make a noise. Someone at the house would ring the dinner bell, telling all their friends that they were through with their corn. An extra good dinner or supper, as the case might be, would be cooked, and everyone had at least one whole day's rest. Even the mules got this one day without working.

Another little saying of my father's helped us remember what happened when you waited too long to plant your corn:

> In July, corn knee-high,
> In August, he layed it by,
> In September there came a big frost.
> Now you see what corn this young
> man lost.

Fodder also had to be saved. All the blades from where the ear of corn grew down were stripped from the stalk, leaving the one on which the corn grew. Every few handfuls were placed between two stalks close to the ground; here they would cure out. After a few days, these would be tied into bundles, and stacked in a shock, or hauled to the barn. The remaining stalk was cut off just above the ear of corn, and tied into bundles and placed together in smaller shocks. These were called "tops" and were not as valuable as the blade fodder. The tops were usually fed to the cows, and the rest kept for the horses. Taking care of fodder was one work I could never do. I know now I was allergic to the smell, though I did not know what was wrong then. I just knew I always got sick when I pulled fodder or cut tops, but it never seemed to bother me once it was cured out, and I could help put it away.

My father's generation had no glass jars, so they did not can fruits or vegetables. They filled large crocks or churns with applebutter. When boiled down very stiff and sweetened with molasses, it would keep fresh for many weeks. Big barrels were filled with smoked apples; a few holes were made in the bottom of the barrel so the juice would run out, then filled up a few inches with apples that had been pared and sliced, with the core removed. On top of these a dish was placed in which a small amount of sulfur was slowly burned by placing a heated piece of iron inside the dish. A quilt over the top kept the smoke from escaping. Next day, another layer of apples and more sulfur was burned and so on, until the barrel was full. The sulfur gave the apples an "off" flavor that took a little getting used to, but was supposed to be good for you. I loved the taste myself, and always served them topped with blackberry jelly.

The late apples could be "holed away" in the ground. Often the floor of the house was removed and the hole dug there. It was lined with straw, the apples were poured in, and more straw and dirt were mounded over the top. You had to be very careful that none of these apples were bruised or rotten. Some were kept in barrels, each wrapped separately in a piece of paper. Sweet potatoes were also kept this way. Many times these barrels were left all winter in a corner of the bedroom, hid from view by a curtain or quilt. Apples were fried, or made into pies and dumplings.

Peaches were canned in syrup. We had a "cling stone" peach, so small that the stone could not be removed as in other peaches. Often we would peel these and can them whole—the stone gave them a very nice flavor—sometimes using sugar, and some in sugar, vinegar, and spice. We had a few pears, and I remember my sister, Frances, had a quince tree. Some folks, not many, had cherries and plums, but almost everyone had a gooseberry patch, and strawberries grew wild in many places. We picked and canned huckleberries and raspberries, but we used blackberries the most; from these we made jelly and jam. Dumplings were made by bringing the sweetened, cooked berries to a boil and dropping in fist-sized balls of biscuit dough.

Berry "sass" was a breakfast dish. The boiling berries were thickened with a little flour and water—not quite as heavy as the sauce used for a pie filling—sweetened and served like a pudding. I always loved to pick berries. No one ever went alone, because of snakes. The huckleberries grew on the tops of ridges. Every year, when they began to ripen, someone would start a rumor that a bear or wildcat had been seen on such and such a hollow, or maybe the story would be that some crazy man or desperate criminal was loose. Moonshiners started these tales so as to scare the women. They were afraid the women would find the moonshine stills while hunting huckleberries.

No one picks berries anymore; almost all the old orchards are gone. Of the fourteen apple trees that grew in my yard when I moved here, only four remain, too old for fruit, giving little shade, and almost dangerous to let stand. In fact, during the severe cold weather this past winter we reopened our fireplace, and chopped one of our apple trees into firewood. I almost felt like I was forsaking an old friend.

All fruits and berries were eaten raw, or cooked in syrup, and made into jelly and jam, but most were used for dumplings or pies. For peach cobbler the slices were baked with layers of biscuit dough. Apples were used in fried pies, apples or applebutter, folded into small thin sheets of dough and fried in deep fat. I have also heard these called half-moon pies or moccasin pies. We also used vinegar as a substitute for fruit, making pies or dumplings flavored with vinegar, sugar and spice. A "barefoot dumpling" was when the balls of dough were cooked in boiling water, containing only salt and lard. Of course, they were better in chicken broth or fresh meat "sop."

We grew corn for feed and bread, but we also used it as a vegetable, canning it and pickling it in brine salt water for winter use, while the kernels were still young enough to be soft. Pickled corn is good fried in a little sugar, but it's best to eat as a snack, sitting around the fire at night and biting it directly off the cob. "Gritted bread" (probably from the word grater) was made from young corn; a gritter was made by driving holes in a piece of tin, maybe an empty peach can, with a nail, then fastening the tin to a board. The ears of corn were rubbed over the sharp edges made by the nail holes, to make meal. If the corn was young enough, no water needed to be added, just a little salt and baking soda, baked in a greased pan. Eaten with sweet milk, it was a meal in itself. You can use corn to grit until it gets old enough to shell from the cob. After the juice or "milk" on the inside of the grains begins to dry, the water must be added, to make a soft dough before baking.

I guess of all vegetables, beans were used the most. There were many kinds of seeds, from the "bunch" beans grown in the garden, to field beans planted along with the corn. The stalks of corn make a place for the bean vines to grow. Beans were pickled in brine salt water in large wooden barrels. We also canned them. Many times we placed the closed glass jars full of beans in a washtub filled with water allowing them to cook for several hours on a fire outside.

Then there was a "tough" bean. The hull was too hard to eat. These were used for soup beans, cooked by themselves or mixed with the dried beans. Salt pork or hog's jowl was added to the beans while they cooked. A friend once told me how every night, before being allowed to go to bed, he and his brothers and sisters each had to shell enough beans to fill a large cup.

We always raised two crops of cabbage. The later one was planted in early July in the hill and not transplanted. These were "holed away" for winter use. A long trench, or "fur," was made with the plow. The fully grown cabbages were pulled up "by the roots," with a few of the bottom leaves broken off. The remaining excess leaves were wrapped around the "head" and placed side by side with the roots turned up in the hole made by the plow; then dirt was thrown up around the cabbages, leaving part of the stalk and the roots exposed. This way they were easily found and removed. They would stay all winter and keep fresh. Cabbages kept this way have a sweet wholesome flavor that you can get no other way, and far exceeds anything you can buy in the supermarket.

And then, of course, there was sauerkraut: cabbage pickled in salt. I also use a little sugar and vinegar. We now put kraut in glass jars, but "back then" we used large churns or crocks or wooden barrels. Our folks would sometimes put the cabbages in the barrel whole, a layer at a time, and cut them up with a shovel. (I have known of people that dried cabbage. I remember watching an old man, when I lived at Dwarf, drying cabbage leaves on his housetop. I never did eat any.)

Beets were cooked and canned in sugar, spice, water, and vinegar; they were eaten no other way. We served them with shucky beans or as a snack. I love to pickle boiled eggs in the liquid where the beets were cooked; the bright red color makes the eggs pretty and gives them a nice flavor. This is a must at Easter for my family.

Tomatoes were thought to be poison by our grandmothers, and were raised only as a flower. We canned the ripe ones to be used in vegetable soup; some added sugar and used it for dessert. Of course, during the summer they were sliced and served with green beans, or added to slaw. Green tomatoes are good sliced, rolled in meal, to which a little salt and pepper is added, and fried in deep fat. My husband likes them sweetened, I don't. There is a small variety which we call "tommy toes." Green tomatoes were also canned in sugar, spice, and vinegar, sometimes by themselves, sometimes with peppers, cabbage, and other vegetables. We also mixed green tomatoes, green pepper, and green cabbage, and pickled them in brine salt water; we called this "pickle lilly" or "chow chow." No matter what you called it—fried in grease and eaten with beans and corn bread—it was good. We ate corn bread for at least two meals each day. Very few people do this anymore. It's easier to use the toaster, I guess.

Next to the beans, I guess more potatoes were used. They were "kelp over" by holing them away. They were "fried, baked, cooked, roasted in the ashes under the grate, added to soup, and boiled with their jackets on." Sometimes we would take them to school with us and boil them in an empty lard bucket, on the coal heating stove. The teacher would help us eat them at recess.

We "bedded" our sweet potatoes in a "hot bed" made from shucks, manure, and dirt, and covered with fodder and an old quilt. After they began sprouting. the fodder and quilt were removed. When large enough, the plants were then transplanted to hills or ridges. Sweet potatoes were baked, roasted, fried in sugar and lard, or cooked with some salt and sugar added. We canned them by cooking them in jars, like the beans. We kept them through the winter in barrels or boxes, each wrapped separately in a piece of paper.

Sweet peppers were eaten raw; stuffed with sausage and other meats; canned in sugar, spice, water and vinegar; mixed with other vegetables to make "pickle lilly" or mixed pickles. Hot pepper or strong pepper was eaten as an additive to other vegetables. We also canned it in vinegar, or strung it up on twine, and allowed it to dry for winter use. Some folks like it added to fresh meat when cooked. We put a few pods of hot pepper on the top of our barrels or churns of salt pickles. It kept the gnats from bothering them, and also gave a good flavor. We added red hot pepper to our paste when we were lining our houses with newspaper and magazines. This kept the mice from eating the paste and ruining the paper. I remember once I had made a large kettle of paste from flour and water, to which I had added a large amount of pepper. I had set it on the back of the stove to cool. One of my boys come in from school, took a large spoonful, thinking it was his supper. It really gave him a hot mouth; I was sorry for him, but I had to laugh. He said he knew why the mice refused to eat it.

Cushaw and "punkins" were planted in the corn, every fourth hill, every fourth row. The small ones were fed to the hogs or cows. The hard-shell cushaws were chopped into small chunks and cooked, then placed in a pan, covered with sugar and spice, and baked. The soft-shell ones were peeled, sliced, cooked and mashed with sugar and spice to make cushaw butter. Some folks added cooked cushaw or pumpkin to their cornmeal dough, and baked it. "Molassie bread" was made this way also. Cushaws are better if molasses is substituted for sugar. And, of course, there were "punkin pies." Many cushaws and pumpkins, along with squashes, were dried. A green pole was hung by strings over the open fireplace. The cushaws were sliced into large circles or rings, then hung on this pole. In a few days they were dried, and more were hung up. This way they could be preserved for winter use, cooked with sugar and lard, or maybe salt pork or hog's jowl—very good. I have seen bushels of dried cushaws and "punkins" hung up in the smokehouse in the winter. By spring, it would have all been eaten.

Asparagus was only grown as a shrub in the yard, never eaten. The full-grown bush, with its green fernlike leaves and bright seed pod, is very beautiful. I have heard the old folks say, "You know, there are folks who eat 'sparegrass' when the sprouts are little." Yet, I never knew of anyone trying it.

Artichokes to us are the potatolike roots of a tall plant that have beautiful yellow flowers that resemble daisies. They were only eaten raw, as a snack.

Cucumbers were sweet-pickled and canned, used with other vegetables for "mixed pickles," pickled in brine salt, eaten raw, sliced and served with green beans or slaw.

Peas were one of the earliest seeds to be planted, sometimes as early as February. We grew a tender-hull kind that could be cooked like string beans, hull and all. We very seldom shelled them. Peas are delicious cooked together with very small young potatoes.

We grew two crops of turnips: a few were planted in ridges for summer use, and then in the fall we planted a larger crop, "broadcasting" the seed over the now empty garden. The tops were cooked for greens; the roots were holed away or put in the cellar. The cold weather does not hurt turnips; they keep growing almost all winter. I like to cook them together—the tops and roots—when the turnips are small.

Rhubarb we called "pie plants." Every garden had a long row, used for pies or dumplings, fried as apples, or mixed with strawberries to make jelly. It "came in" just as most of the winter food was used up, and the new garden was still too young to use. It was supposed to be good for you and help to cure "spring fever."

Some of us grew a few gourds just for the fun of it, but our forefathers grew them to be used. The larger ones would hold lard, salt, soft soap, meal, molasses, or whatever. The small, long-handled ones were water dippers. We called the small round egg-shaped kind "hen foolers," because we used them for nest eggs.

There were many different kinds of onions. Fall and winter onions grew through the winter, and could be eaten green. "Tater onions" got their name for the way the new ones grew in a cluster around the old one; they were kept for the roots. "Spring shallots" were very early and very small.

Onions were eaten as a dish, not an additive. They were fried either while green or after grown, but not as "onion rings," as they are now prepared. To keep for winter, they were pulled while there was still some top remaining, tied in bunches, and hung from nails in the barn or smokehouse. They become better after being allowed to freeze. Onions were used as a medicine, roasted, mashed and made into a "pollus" placed on the chest, to help "break up" a cold. Onion soup was also used for a cold or tonsillitis.

Then there were wild greens or "salet." There are many different kinds; sometimes the same plant was known by a different name by different people. "Plantin" is the one used most, a small thick-leafed green with a very distinct flavor, a little like cabbage. Then for cooking there was "sheep's leg," "groundhog ear," and "speckled dock." Poke salet had to be used very carefully, because it could be poison; it was cooked in one water, washed and cooked again, then fried in a lot of lard. If eaten too often, it can become a laxative. The stalks were also good peeled, rolled in meal, and fried. "Crow's foot," "shoestring," "chicken salet," and "creases" were eaten raw, cut up, sprinkled with salt, and then "killed" by pouring real hot grease over them.

In my father's time hogs were allowed to run wild. Each man had a "mark" so as to tell his own. The pig's ear was either notched or split, some used both, but no two exactly alike. When a sow mothered a "gang" of pigs, if the owner did not catch the small ones and mark them before they were weaned, and they had quit running with the mother, they were then accepted as "wild pigs": anyone who caught them was the owner. He could put his mark on them or butcher them for food. Wild hogs grew very fat on "mast": nuts and roots they found in the woods. I thought this gave the meat a good flavor, but I have talked with some folks that said this was not so; they were better if brought in and fed corn a few weeks before butchering them.

The older generations used more beef and sheep for meat than we did, but chicken and dumplings was counted the best dish of any. I have seen my folks cook as many as sixteen grown hens at one time, in an old-fashioned iron "mink" kettle, when there was a big crowd at a wedding, funeral, or family get-together.

Our folks on Caney, in the past, had plenty of good wholesome food. I don't see how they ever ate all these many barrels, holes, cans, and sacks full of beans, corn, cabbage, and many other fruits and vegetables that they called "sass." But they did. Maybe they knew nothing about vitamins or a balanced diet, but they worked hard to grow and put away food.

My father taught me to love nature's beauty as well as her

benefits. I remember how he would listen to the thunder. He would say, "God wouldn't want any of his children to get scared at something He made." I have always loved to listen to the thunder.

He also loved to look at the pretty sunset and rainbows. He often would call me to come outside to enjoy the view with him. The valley would be lit up with bright colors, as the sun set behind the hills. And he would say, "This is the way Eden must have looked before sin entered the world." He would not have known what you meant if you had mentioned any of the masterpieces of paintings. But he enjoyed the pictures painted by the greatest Master of them all. There is nothing more beautiful than a rainbow that seems to form a bridge from one hilltop to the other, or the snow-covered world early in the morning, before man has destroyed it by making paths. The many colors of the autumn leaves remind me of my "crazy quilts," such a blending of colors that the absence of any scheme or pattern makes a beauty or system all its own: a picture you will never forget if you have seen it once.

CHAPTER THIRTEEN

IN MY FATHER'S time, dinner bells were a necessity.
Kitteneye and his neighbors used them for everything from
celebrating election returns to telling the family that dinner
was ready. We soon learned the different tones of each bell
and could tell just who was ringing it by the sound it made.
The children were not allowed to ring it just for fun except
on Christmas; then everyone rang their bell. There was one
old man who every Christmas morning, "let off a blast."
The night before he went up on the hill above his house,
bored a hole in a tree, and filled the hole with gunpowder
and a fuse. Then early Christmas morning, he climbed the
hill and lit the fuse. We were all awakened by this loud noise,
rang our bells, and shot firecrackers. I guess there is
nowhere in the world where folks celebrate Christmas with
fireworks, except here in the hills. It's now a violation to use
or sell fireworks, but it has not stopped us. Every Christmas
our hills ring with the sound.

The birth of a new baby was another glad time for using

the bell. What a time to have a party! That was one occasion when the women took over. No men were allowed; even the father must leave home after bringing the "granny" and letting the kinfolks know. This happy time was known as a "Granny Frolic," and the expecting mother prepared for it in advance by making piles of gingerbread and fattening some frying chickens. In some homes there would be a few pints of moonshine. Every married woman friend and relative was welcome; no young girls were permitted. Anyway they were needed at home to look after the small children and menfolks. After the baby was born, bathed, and powdered with powder made from dry clay taken from between the rocks in the chimney, someone would remove the ax from under the bed. (It had been put there to cut the pains.) After ringing the dinner bell to let everyone know the baby was born and both mother and child were alright, the party began. They always cut up the father's hat, if he had not hidden it. I don't know why—maybe it was supposed to bring good luck.

Mountain children knew nothing about a stork; they were taught that babies "were brung by the Hoot Owl." In the evening when the owl began to call "who, who," the children thought he was saying who wants a baby. They would all run out in the yards and answer, "We do, we do." Maybe that's why our families are so large. Nowhere will you find people who love their children more than we do. No matter how large the family or small the house and income, a new arrival is welcome and loved.

Mountain men show a lot of respect for a pregnant woman. It's a law that if a woman asks for help when her baby is due, a man cannot refuse. Once a friend of mine used this to her advantage. She and her husband were "makin' moonshine." They had a large washtub full of the finished product sitting on their kitchen floor and were adding the spring water to "temper" it. Then they poured it into half-gallon mason fruit jars, ready for sale. The woman went to the door to see if everything was alright, and "fer down the holler" she saw the sheriff coming. She was very frightened, and very pregnant. She told her husband to be very quiet. She knew what to do. When the sheriff came to the door, she went outside and met him—looking just as large as she could—and said, "Oh, am I glad you came. I am here by myself, and my baby is being born. Will you please go git Granny for me?"

"Shore. Where does she live?" he answered, never suspecting a lie.

"About half a mile down the creek. Any'un can tell you where, and please hurry."

"Want me to tell any of your kinfolks?"

"No, she's my mother-in-law."

When the sheriff left, the husband begin to carry the whiskey outside and hide it in the "tater hole." He worked as fast as he could but there were still ten jars left on the kitchen floor when they saw the sheriff returning. He had made a fast trip.

"What will we do?" the poor husband wanted to know. His wife got into the bed and said, "Put those jars here with me." He placed them up and down by her side and then covered them with the quilt and made a fast retreat out the back door just in time.

The sheriff had a search warrant; he looked everywhere for whiskey except in the tater hole and in the bed. A few weeks later he ran into the husband at the courthouse and asked him, "Oh say, which was it, a boy or a girl?" He did not know why everyone laughed when the other man answered, "Oh, a gal, in fact, there were five gals."

Everyone in the hills, if they made whiskey or not, "hated the law," especially revenuers. They all joined together to outdo them when one was seen coming. The person who saw him quit whatever he or she was doing and quickly began ringing the dinner bell. "Dong-dong-dong," then a small pause, and then three times again, never stopping until they heard an answering bell from the next neighbor. That neighbor did the same until he heard the next bell. In a very short time the news had traveled up and down every hollow, giving the moonshiners time to get away and hide.

There were small bells worn on a leather strap by the cows and sheep, and one with a short handle that the teacher rang to "take up books." With all these bells you would think that we would have had a church bell, but us mountain folks have a different feeling about our way of worship—very hard to explain to outsiders. Maybe what my father said will help a little: "We don't need a bell to tell us to come to church, for that call is heard with the heart, not the ears."

CHAPTER FOURTEEN

UNCLE JOHN (SUMMER) Slone ran a small grocery store near the mouth of Short Fork. He was a very small man and as long back as I can remember him, he was drawn over in his back, so crippled with rheumatism that he could scarcely walk. But he kept his wife and kids and "lived good" from what he made in his small store.

My Uncle Milton Owens had the next store, near the mouth of Hollybush. Every two weeks a salesman or a "drummer," as we then called them, would come from Paintsville, Kentucky. Verne Stumbo, a very good friend of mine who is now dead, was a drummer. All his life he came riding a mule and carrying large saddle bags filled with his salesbooks and samples. It took him all week to visit the stores up the many small hollows in his territory. I guess he spent the night in the only hotel in Hindman. But he always ate dinner with some of his customers. I also ran a store for many years and he was still a drummer, but by that time we had a rough sort of road and he drove a car.

After the drummer took his orders back to Paintsville, the groceries or goods were shipped by freight to the depot at Wayland. From there they had to be brought in on a wagon.

My father's job was to take his wagon and team of mules and meet the train, every two weeks, to bring this load of groceries for Uncle John. He had to start long before it was daylight and never returned until after dark, for it was a long journey and mules have to rest every now and then when they have a very heavy load. Some weeks he would have to make two trips. If the groceries were left too long in the depot, he would have to pay a "storage charge." So he tried to meet the train.

During the summer my father would also take a load of vegetables and fruits with him to sell to the folks who lived in and around the coal mining camps in Wayland, Lackey, Punkin Center, Garrett, and Glow. Some of the things that he peddled were from the surplus his own family had grown. But much of it was bought from his neighbors. Sometimes a wooden coop was nailed to the back end of the wagon and filled with young frying chickens.

The stuff was loaded on the wagon the night before and he would get up real early and start on his trip. There were lots of other folks who were doing the same thing, and of course the folks were going to buy what they needed from the first "peddling" wagon who came to their door.

On one particular day he was real early, and he thought to himself, "I have got here before anybody else; I will have good luck in sellin' all my load soon." But he was very surprised when no one would buy anything. Up and down, between the rows of houses he went, knocking on door after door. He sold no food that day except to the doctor's wife and the people who lived in the best and richest homes that the bosses of the mines owned.

He could not understand why no one would buy anything. The day before had been payday at the mines. He knew everyone had plenty of money. His vegetables were fresh and good, and he knew no one had been there before him to have sold to them.

At last he came to a little old shack where an old black woman lived all by herself. He had often given her some of his vegetables for free. This day he stopped before her door and called, "Aunt Mary, come out here. I got something fer ye." And going to the back of his wagon, he caught one of the young chickens, and when she came to the door he gave it to her.

"'Lo, Kitteneye," she said. "It has been many a year since I have had a fryin' chicken—not since my old man got mashed up in the mines. I see ye han't sold much of ye stuff today, and I am a'goin' to tell ye why. Ye know ye fellers allus go down to the side of the river and dump what ye don't sell."

This was true, because they had so many vegetables and fruits at home, it wasn't worth the trouble to haul them back, and anyway, he had to have an empty wagon so as to return with Uncle John's "goods" from the depot.

"Well," Aunt Mary went on, "these trifling folks allus goes down there and gits the stuff and takes it home and eats it. They all made up that they would not buy anything today, and then ye would have to dump ye whole load. Don't let on I told ye, or they would be awful mad to me. But ye are allus good to me Kitteneye and I wanted ye to know."

"Well," he said, "I'll have to dump my whole load, but they won't git any fun atter eatin' it."

He went to the store and bought two gallons of kerosine or lamp oil. After unloading his wagon, he poured the oil over all the fruits and vegetables—except what he gave to old Aunt Mary.

Next week when he brought another peddling wagon, everyone was eager to buy from him.

Jim "Summer" Slone and his wife, Frankie Slone

Grandpa Vince Owens and his wife, Lucinda Owens

Right. This picture was taken of my father and mother
about 1905. The building in the back is the schoolhouse
where my sister Flora Belle taught. In the back row are
Vince Slone, Morrell Slone, Flora Belle Slone Fugate, and
Arminda Slone Thomas. In the front are Frances Slone
Jacobs, Isom "Kitteneye" Slone, Devada Slone, Sarah
Slone, Edna Slone Pratt, and Lorenda Slone.

This photo was taken around 1885. In the first row are Liz Slone, Nancy Owens Slone, Beth Slone, Sally Lee Slone, Elizabeth Lee Slone, Phoebe Jane Lee Slone, someone I don't know, and Margaret "Sis" Sparkman. In the second row are "Fat" Isom Slone and (third from left) Preacher Johnny Slone. The woman with her hand over her eyes is my husband's grandmother, Fairy Slone. The old man in the right-hand corner is Grandpa Owens. At his left is my half-brother Cleveland.

Verna Mae at nine months old

Verna Mae with niece Irene

Left. This is the house where I was born. It was built in 1802 by Shady Slone, my great-great-grandfather. My great-grandfather Billie Slone lived here and it became my grandfather's, Jim Slone's, in 1876. My father bought it in 1901 and lived here and then gave it to my brother, Vince Slone, in 1923. It was torn down and moved from the mouth of Trace and rebuilt at the mouth of Short Fork. Some of the logs are still in use in a barn.

Kitteneye Slone and Morrell Slone, making chairs for Mrs. Lloyd

Left. Miss Constance, a nurse who was on Caney between
1916 and 1922. She is riding Little Beck, my father's mule.
She often borrowed him when her work took her up the
hollows and across the hills. Some of the women criticized her
for riding "astraddle"; our womenfolk most always rode
behind their men, using a quilt or blanket for a cushion, or
else they used a sidesaddle.

Kitteneye Slone

CHAPTER FIFTEEN

VERY FEW OF our mountain folks ever stole anything. If you went by a man's apple tree, turnip or watermelon patch, and you took some, it was not counted as stealing, it was the custom. Anyone was more than welcome to what he could eat that belonged to his neighbor. Of course, like everything else there were a few exceptions.

My father owned a little black mule named "Little Beck." He had raised him from a colt. He was almost like one of the family and as gentle as a kitten. He would come from anywhere in the pasture when he heard my father whistle for him.

One evening one of my cousins and her boyfriend, Dick Patton, came to stay all night with us. The girls were very pleased, for we had few visitors and they thought a lot of their cousin.

Papa did not think it strange when Dick offered to go help him feed the stock and milk the cow. This was a common rule. If you were visiting anyone, you helped with the chores. But he knew why the next morning when he got up, for Dick and his girlfriend were gone. So was Little Beck.

My father began asking the close neighbors if they had heard anything during the night. He soon learned enough to know they had gone toward Wayland.

When he stopped at Joanar Slone's and learned someone had stolen a saddle from him during the night, he knew he was on the right track. When he reached Wayland, he heard that a man and a woman bearing the description of the two he was after had gotten aboard the train going toward Allen. He knew they had sold Little Beck to someone near Wayland. He began going from farmhouse to farmhouse giving the whistle that he had taught his mule to answer. It was almost evening. Tired and worried, he had almost given up, until at last from a stall, away down in a hollow, he heard an answer to his call. He ran to the barn and looked through the cracks between the logs, and sure enough, there was his mule.

The man who had bought the mule refused to give him up. My father came back with the sheriff and a warrant. Kitteneye gave a complete description of his mule even to the few white hairs on his left hip. All the rest of his body was black. The sheriff looked on the mule's hip and could not find the white hairs. My father took his hand and ruffled the hairs up, and sure enough, there were the stubs of white hairs, showing where they had been cut off. The law gave Little Beck back to his rightful owner and put out a twenty-five dollar reward for the arrest of the thieves.

A few weeks later my father and another man, both sworn in as deputies, learned where the two were staying and surprised them one morning while they were still in bed. When my cousin saw who it was she said, "You know you han't goin' to arrest me, are you Uncle Kitteneye?"

"Don't you uncle me now," he said. "You fergit I was your kinfolk when you helped steal my mule. You rode Little Beck then, you can ride behind me now to the jailhouse." But he must have forgiven her because Dick was the only one who went to jail and I think he escaped and was never heard of around here anymore.

At his trial, the judge asked Dick if he stole Kitteneye's mule and he answered, "No, I stole his bridle and the mule happened to have its head in it."

It seems as if every family clan had at least one "bad man," but I think many had more fame than their just due. The only one that had any connection with my life was Bad Amos Fugate, or Little Amos, as he was called by his friends—and he had many more friends than enemies. The story goes that his sister had a fight with some neighbor woman, and the other woman was killed. Amos confessed to the crime to save his sister and was sentenced to prison. Before his sentence was up, he dressed in women's clothes and walked out with some visitors. A price was placed on his head, to be brought in "dead or alive." Whenever he saw one of these posters he would mark out the word "alive," saying that he would have to be killed before captured.

He was a cousin to my brother-in-law, Sam Fugate, and a very good friend. My sister and their children really loved Amos. They helped him by giving him food while he was hiding from the law.

One day my father was going to visit his daughter, Flora Fugate. As he was going across the hill to Ball, where she then lived, he came upon a group of men sitting by the narrow bridle path. The men were drinking and playing cards. My father said he was upon them before he knew who they were. He said he was really scared when he recognized one of them as Amos Fugate. At first he considered the idea of turning back, but then thought better of that. The men moved back out of the path and let him ride on by. Just as he thought he was getting out of sight and all was well, Amos called and said, "Hey, are you Kitteneye?"

My father turned back and said, "Yes." Amos said, "Come back here a minute." Father really got scared then, but he turned his mule around and went back.

"Did you want a drink of good corn liquor?"

"Shore would." And Amos handed him his bottle.

"Do you know who I am?" Amos asked.

"Yeah, I think I do," Father replied.

"Well, you are Flora's paw, so go on, and don't tell a livin' soul you saw us here." And Father promised.

That night after supper at Flora's house, and after Father had gone to bed, Amos came to the door. Sam let him in and gave him his supper. Amos asked Flora if my father told them about seeing him, and he laughed when she said no. "Well, I didn't mean for him to not tell you, but I guess when I said to tell no one, he sure meant to keep his promise."

A few days later, Amos was coming back to visit Sam again, and some men "lay waid" him and riddled his body with bullets from a machine gun. His own folks kept the killers from getting his body, then they guarded his grave for one year, keeping a lighted lantern sitting on his tombstone at night, with a "'round the clock" guard. Those bounty hunters received no reward.

CHAPTER SIXTEEN

THERE MUST STILL have been a few Indians living in this part of Kentucky when our first settlers came—and a few intermarriages. The Thomases and the Mosleys both are proud to lay claim to being part Indian, and the look of this Indian blood still shows up in some of their appearances. My own granddaughter has the long black hair, high cheek-bones, dark eyes, and stately way of walking that would remind anyone of an Indian princess. I know I see her through the love of a grandmother's eyes, but she is still a pretty girl to anyone.

The story I want to tell is about an old Thomas man who showed how much like the Indians he was in his ability to walk for many miles without "givin' out."

In those early days the closest courthouse was at Catlettsburg, Kentucky. My father and a few of his friends were to appear there in a famous murder trial as witnesses. Mr. Thomas was one of these men. They had all agreed to meet at Hindman, so as to make the journey together.

Everyone was there, riding their mules or horses. When Mr. Thomas came walking, one of the men asked him where his horse was. He quietly answered, "I am going to walk." All the men gave a loud laugh and told him he should know better, that no man could walk that many miles, and if he did, he would be too late for the trial that was only three days away. Mr. Thomas said, "I bet I can walk as fast as any horse you got. I will keep up with any of you." One of the men who was very proud of his horse called the bet and started out. The man walked beside the horse. My father and the rest of his friends followed, but they did not catch up with the two men until nightfall, when they reached a town where they all had agreed on staying together for the night. They found Mr. Thomas calmly eating his supper as if he was not one bit tired. But the horse the man had ridden was not as strong as the "part-Indian" walker, because the next morning the horse was found dead in its stall. Mr. Thomas finished the rest of the trip walking fast enough to keep up with the crowd and was always, after that, referred to as the "man who walked a horse to death."

Something else happened on their way back that my father loved to tell. As folks made these long journeys, they would stop along the way to get water to drink. Sometimes it would be at some cabin, where they were always welcome because visitors were so few and people were always glad to hear any news. In many places the roads would only be "bridle paths" through the woods. Then there would be springs of water where the men would bend over and drink without any cup, drawing the water into their mouth, somewhat like animals do.

When my father and his friends were coming back from Catlettsburg, the day was very hot and they were all very thirsty. Just as they were coming around the bend in the road, there stood an old woman beside a spring of water. She had just dipped her bucket full of water and started back to her cabin. The men stopped and asked her for some of her water and she answered, "Shore."

My father said he looked at her, and she was so dirty her clothes and face were covered with soot and grime, and tobacco juice was dribbling from the corners of her mouth. He wanted the water so badly, but the thought of placing his lips on the side of the drinking gourd where he knew her mouth had been several times, made him feel almost sick. So when it came his time to take a drink, he turned the gourd upside down and drank from the hole in the handle. As he handed the gourd back to her she said, "Well, I declare, you are the first man I ever did see that drunk water out of a gourd like I do."

CHAPTER SEVENTEEN

FROM THE RECORDS of old deeds I have found with their names, I know my mother and father lived in different places on Caney. Only once in my mother's lifetime did my father move his family "off of Caney."

In the years around 1895 they lived on Bunyun, where I now live, in fact in the same house where my husband and I first lived. Three of her children were born under the same roof where my two oldest were born. I love to think when I am working in my garden, "This is the very same soil my mother once turned over with her hoe." There used to be an Old Belle Flower apple tree in the yard my mother set out. I got a double pleasure using those apples, as I was sharing something with a mother I never had.

In the year 1899, my sister Jezzie Ann died at the age of two, just a few months after my mother had lost another premature baby. My father was gone from home and the older kids buried the small child on the hillside across from my home. Losing Jezzie Ann so close after this other tragedy upset my mother very much. My father thought it would help her if he could get her away from all the unpleasant memories. He swapped land with one of his brothers and moved to Possum Trot. But this only made matters worse. So in 1901 he bought the old family home from his father and moved to the mouth of Trace, close to the family graveyard. There they remained until my mother's death.

Around 1930, my father, stepmother and I moved to Dwarf, a distance of less than thirty miles, but in that day and time, it seemed like a long way.

We loaded our "house plunder" on wagons pulled by mules and drove to Hindman. There it was loaded on a truck and taken to Bear Branch, and then up the hollow in sleds. We loaded the wagons the night before and started long before daylight. I remember eating dinner just outside of Hindman, from a bucket. We had packed and brought along boiled eggs, fried side meat, corn bread, and onions. When we drive through there now, I try to remember how it looked then. We sat there on the side of the creek, drinking water from a spring, feeding and resting the mules, visiting with everyone that passed. After sharing our lunch, the men with the wagons returned home and we went on with the truck.

I never will forget that first night at Dwarf in our new home. The house was little more than a barn, one room about twelve-feet square, with a chimney made from picked-up creek rocks, and the logs of the walls nothing but poles. We had bought the place from a Emery Halland, who wanted to sell so as to move to the coal mines at Harlan. My father was building a new house, but he wanted to move before cold weather, so we lived in this shack for a few weeks until the new house was finished. That first night, there was only time to put up one bed, so I slept on some fodder placed on the floor with quilts, sheets, and pillows. I was awakened the next morning when an old mule began pulling the fodder through the cracks between the small logs of the wall of the house.

When my father and my brother-in-law Sam Fugate got three sides of the new house finished, we moved in. The old house had to be torn down to make room for the new one's fourth side. Before a chimney could be made, cold weather set in. I remember my father kept a large fire made of logs in the yard, and believe it or not, it kept us warm, even though the house was open on one side. The only thing was, we had to take turns sleeping, so as to guard the fire.

I had never seen such big trees as those that grew on Bear Branch; the woods on Caney had been timbered out a long time before I was born. My brother-in-law and my sister owned almost half of the hollow. He had bought a saw mill and was cutting the logs and selling the lumber to some of the mining camps. Everytime I think of these years, I can still hear the hum of that saw and recall the smell of the sawdust, in which my nieces and I used to play.

He had several men to help him. Some cut trees, some worked at the mill, while others drove the teams that hauled the finished lumber to the mouth of the hollow, where it was picked up by trucks. Many of these men boarded with my sister. Some were blacks. The white men slept in the house with the family, but the blacks had a small shack close to the mill. They all ate together. The table was not large enough for everyone, so first the white men ate, then the blacks, and last of all the family. There was a hired girl, whose last name was Richie. How that girl could sing! The girls would help her do the dishes, if she would sing for us. When she got tired—because we never got through listening—she would say, "Sing a little song, won't take long. Duddle up, duddle up. Now it's all gone." We knew it was all over for the night.

I don't think my father was ever completely satisfied at Dwarf. He moved back to Caney, then back to Dwarf so many times that it became a family joke. Once he said he had made the move so many times that the chickens had gotten so they would "lay down on their backs and cross their legs so as to be ready to be tied." And once he asked my brother Vince to help him with his wagon and mule, and Vince told him, "Well, Paw, I am kind of busy this week with making my molasses. You get some of the others to help you. I will be free next week and help you move back."

CHAPTER EIGHTEEN

SOMETIME BETWEEN 1901, when my father moved his family to the old home place at the mouth of Trace, and the year 1909, when my sister Alverta was born, a large lumber company named Cole and Crain came to Caney Creek to buy up all the trees that were eighteen inches in diameter "or up."

Their foreman's name was Hayes Johnson. He built a shanty at the mouth of Hollybush for those men who lived too far away to go home at night. He also had a store and sold dry goods and notions (I don't think he sold groceries) near the shanty.

He had the men that he hired to work for him build a dam just below where the waters from Caney and Hollybush meet. Then they built a "trom road" from the dam up to the mouth of Trace. Here it branched out and became two tracks—one going up Trace as far as Bill Owens', and the other up Caney onto Short Fork. It ended where Short Fork is divided into two different branches of water. Henry C. Short lived there.

This trom road was made somewhat like a small railroad track. Logs about four feet long were placed about every two or three feet on the roadway, in a straight line. Then running lengthwise along the top of each tie the rails were "spiked down" with iron spikes. The rails were also made of wood, but had an iron coating on the top side.

The logs were carried to the dam along the trom road on small flat cars, also built of wood, with three wheels on each side. The outside of these wheels were iron, with a groove in the middle to fit on the rails of the trom road.

Each car could carry four or five logs. It was all downgrade from the end of the road to the dam, so there was no power needed to operate them. They did have some kind of a "hand brake" for stopping the cars. I think the empty cars were pulled back up the hills by oxen or mules.

After the water had been caught in the dam and enough logs had been hauled and dumped ready, the gate of the dam was opened and the logs floated to Maytown, where they were then taken by riverboats to Catlettsburg. I don't know where they went from there. There may have been a large sawmill there, or they may have been sent somewhere farther on.

G.C. Huff was living in Trace then and owned several oxen. He and my father hauled most of the logs out of the hills using these "beasts of burden." One of these oxen had an accident that resulted in a broken leg. It was killed and fed to the workers. My father did not approve of this; he said it was "eatin' one of his friends." When the men were called to eat their dinner, they were surprised when Kitteneye expressed a wish to say the blessing. He always said you should give thanks to God every hour of the day from your heart. A memorized prayer repeated automatically came only from the lips and did not please God. Kitteneye's blessing that day may not have met with the approval of his Maker, but it caused the men to laugh:

Poor old steer, what brought you here,
You been beat and banged for many a year,
Beat and banged and given abuse
And now brought up for the table use.

Almost everyone on Caney sold their timber to Hayes Johnson. My father sold his and helped to cut it. Hayes paid so much a cubic foot for the trees and sixty cents each for cutting and hauling them to where they were loaded on the flat cars. This job lasted for five or six years. My sisters said they could remember when my mother sold vegetables and chickens and eggs to Hayes Johnson. He bought them to feed the men who lived in his shanty. In exchange she received cloth and other things from his store. Vada said she could remember that mother "swapped cabbage to the cloth to make the dress she is wearing in the picture I have of her, which is in my living room now."

After Hayes Johnson got all the trees he wanted, and, maybe became a rich man from the profits, he left Caney. Soon the shanty rotted down. The dam was used no more and soon washed away. The trom road was covered over by soil with each new spring flood, or "warsh out" as we mountain folks call it. Another part of Caney's history was forgotten so completely, that when the flood of 1937 uncovered some of the old trom road, many people wondered what it was.

CHAPTER NINETEEN

MY FATHER DID not, nor would he let us believe in ghosts. We called them "haunts" or "buggers," but many of our neighbors would "sware right down to ye" that they had "seed things." There were certain places where more than one person had encountered something that did not comply with the laws of nature, and heard voices or sounds when there was no reason (or so they said). We even still have a Bugger Branch on Caney and a Bugger Hollow just across the hill on Watts Fork. I wonder if any of our old folks really believed these stories. There were many great storytellers. We had few books, and listening to these stories were our only entertainment of this kind. Father would tell us it was alright to listen, but to never tell the person that we did not believe them. When we would hear some "bugger tale" from one of our schoolmates and come home and repeat it to him, he would make a fanning motion with his arms and a blowing with his lips and say, "Now, there, you see, I have blowed it all away. No more bugger."

When he heard or saw something strange he never stopped until he found out what it really was. When he was a child, folks believed a cow could lose her cud. They had noticed how cattle would burp up their food and chew it the second time. They did not understand, and thought the cud was a special thing belonging to cows. If a cow lost this cud they thought it would die. They would make them another from an old dishrag and a salty meat skin, maybe adding something else. This would save the cow's life. One day Father was watching a small calf. His job was to see it did not get into the corn or garden patch. When the calf began to chew its cud, he held its mouth and made it spit it out, to see what it was.

Some of the folks also believed in witches. Some even said they were a witch themselves. To become one you had to go up on a high hill on the first night of a full moon, spread a white sheet on the ground beneath an oak tree, kneel on this sheet, shoot a gun toward the sky, curse the Lord and bless the Devil. Three drops of blood would fall on the sheet. Then you would have the powers of a witch. But when you died you would belong to the Devil.

Once there was this old woman who thought someone had bewitched her cow, causing her milk to "turn" and to taste awful. Father knew the reason was because she was not a very good housekeeper and did not sterilize her churn and milk bucket. So he told her to go to the north side of her spring where she got water, choose three small "gravels" or stones, wash her churn real clean, put the gravels in the bottom, then rinse it with boiling water. This would break the spell.

One story told and believed by some of my husband's folks was about the Devil. Some men had a habit of going to an old lonely shack every Saturday night to play cards, gamble, and drink moonshine whiskey. This one time, about midnight, a stranger rode up on a very fine black horse, hitched it up outside to the fencepost, and came in. He spoke to each one and called each by name, although none knew him. He asked if could he sit in on their poker game. No one refused. Very slowly, as the game went on for hours, he began to win all their money. One man dropped a card on the floor. When he stooped down to pick it up, he saw that the stranger had hooves where there should have been feet. This scared him so much that he jumped up, turning the table over, and ran out the door. All the other men ran after him, leaving all their cards, money, and jugs with the stranger. As they ran out of sight, they heard the stranger laughing, a strange high crackling sound, like the wind through a forest fire. The next day when it was daylight some of the men were a little braver and came back. The shack was burned to the ground. They looked in the ashes and found the silver money, melted and formed into the shape of a cross. None of these men ever played poker again.

One old lady gained a lot of fame because she had a "knocking spirit." Anyone who spent the night with her could hear it, ask it any question, and it would answer two knocks for a no, three for a yes. This was a great mystery, until someone found out that one of her sons had tied a thread spool to a string, and pulled it through a knothole near his bed.

There was another woman who heard a knocking in her loft, every night, three knocks—the second one not as loud as the first, the third one still fainter—only to begin again. She was a "wedder," living by herself. She asked my father to come and find out what this knocking sound was.

Now these old-fashioned lofts were much more than just a space beneath the roof. They were more like a second story to the house—not high enough for a bedstead, but feather beds or straw ticks were placed on the floor for the children or extra company. Some had a stairway that went up by the chimney inside, some, not so nice, had a ladder on the outside. In my father's house, this upstairs was very nice and comfortable, but I remember staying all night with some friends. We had to climb up an outside ladder. There was no shutter to the opening where we went in. The next morning we awoke to find a two-inch snow covering us, where we were warm between two big feather beds and many quilts. I would be scared to death for you, grandchildren, to sleep like that, but we thought it was a lot of fun. We put our clothes on under the covers and hurried, laughing, down to the fire and breakfast.

In these lofts we also kept our dried beans, cushaw, onions, and seed corn. Almost everyone had an old trunk or two full of the dead folk's clothes, and anything else that needed storing away. So it was up in a loft like this that the old woman heard the strange knocking sound. As luck would have it that night the moon was full, not a cloud in the sky. After supper and before dusk, my father went up the ladder and settled himself in a corner. It was very hard for him to keep from going to sleep. The light came in from a small opening where the wind had blown a board off. He thought, "Tomorrow I will nail that back on fer her." He tried counting the rows of boards, the strings of popcorn, the bunches of dried beans. He would first rub one eye, then the other—anything to keep himself awake. He could hear the squeak, squeak, of the old woman's rocking chair. At last there was something moving in the other corner. There was a board across a barrel, probably filled with dried apples. Next to this sat a large churn. Like a flash something ran across this board, made a dive from the end, and landed in the churn. Whack, whack, whack, three times went the other end of the board. He went over and looked into the churn. Mr. Rat gave a fast retreat. The churn had been full of cracklin's, kept there until the "right time of moon" to be made into soap.

When one family went to stay all night with another (as they often did), after supper and the dishes were washed and put away, and all the other "work done up," everyone would get together. We'd gather around the fire, if it was winter, or on the porch, around a "gnat smoke" made by burning rags, if it was summer. The older folks would sit in chairs with the young children in their laps, or huddled around their feet. That's when we would hear all these scary bugger tales. By the time we were ready to go to sleep, it sure was nice to know the small ones would be stuck in at the foot of the grown-up's bed, or so many of us in the same bed that we would have to sleep sideways so as to have room for us all.

These stories lose a lot in being written—the facial expressions, the movement of the hands, the bending forward of the body, the lowering and raising of the voice by the storyteller—cannot be captured on paper. They added much to the enjoyment of listening to these bugger tales.

There was one story my father taught me that I have told my grandchildren so many times I know they will never forget it. It's kind of a poem, or maybe you would call it a chant. There is no end to it, and each line must be followed by a long, low moan:

There was an old woman all skin and bone—mo-o-an
She took a notion she would not stay at home—mo-o-an
She got up—she walked down—mo-o-an
To the village churchyard ground—mo-o-an
She saw the dead a'laying around—mo-o-an
She saw the grave of her only son—mo-o-an
She thought of all the crimes he had done—mo-o-an

And on and on until you had your audience really listening. Then, very suddenly, maybe right in the middle of a word, you would jump and scream *boo*. Even after telling it over and over again, and they knew the loud boo was coming, I would still be able to scare them. Just think what it would do to someone hearing it for the first time.

I think some of the parents used bugger tales to scare their children just to make them be good. It seems as if every family had a "Hairy Mouth" or a "Bloody Bones" that would come and get you if you were not good. My father would not let us be told anything like this. We were taught to be good because that was what Jesus wanted us to do. He told us there was a Devil, but not one you could see with your natural eyes. And so have I taught my dear grandchildren.

Kitteneye knew a lot of fairy stories, some different and some very similar to your versions today. Rumplestiltskin was named Tom Tit Tot, and the girl with the glass slipper was Cinder Ellen. He knew hundreds of songs or rhymes all by heart. I can't recall all of them, but this story would not be complete unless I gave you at least two: "The Bird Song" and "The Fox Song," my favorite ones.

The Fox Song

It was a moon shining night
The stars shining bright
Two foxes went out for to prey.
They trotted along
With frolic and song
To cheer their lonely way.

Through the woods they went
Not a rabbit could they scent
Nor a lonely goose on stray.
Until at last they came

To some better game
A farmer's yard by the way.

On the roost there sat
Some chickens as fat
As foxes could wish for a dinner.
They hunted around
Until a hole they found
And both went in at the center.

They both went in
With a squeeze and a grin
And the chickens they soon were killed.
And one of them lunched
And hunched, and bunched
Until his stomach was fairly filled.

The other more wise
Looked around with both eyes
He would hardly eat at all.
For as he came in
With a squeeze and a grin
He noted the hole was quite small.

The night rolled on
And daylight down
Two men came out with a pole.
Both fox flew
And one went through
But the greedy one stuck in the hole.

The hole he stuck
So full of his pluck
Of the chickens he had been eating.

He could not get out
Or turn about
So he was killed by beating.

The Bird Song

I use to kill birds in my boyhood,
Black ones, robins, and wrens.
I hunted them up on the hillside,
I hunted them down in the glen.

I did not think it was sinful,
I did it only for fun.
I had such sport of royalty,
With the poor little birds and my gun.

One bright day in the springtime,
I saw a brown thrush in a tree.
She was singing so merrily and sweetly,
Just as sweet as a birdy could be.

I raised my gun in a twinkle,
I fired, the aim it was true.
For a moment the little bird fluttered,
Then off to the bushes it flew.

I followed it softly and closely,
And there to my sorrow I found,
Right close to a nest full of young ones,
The mother bird dead on the ground.

The young ones for food they were calling,
Yet how could they ever be fed?
For the dear darling mother who loved them,

Was laying there bleeding and dead.

I picked it up in my anger,
I stroked the motherly bird.
Not never again in my lifetime,
Would I kill a poor innocent bird.

Kitteneye was a good hand at making up his own rhymes
or pieces. I am sorry to say many were about his friends and
neighbors, and he would picture their character so quaint
and real that I would be afraid to repeat them. He used his
imagination in using swear words and expressions. Some of
his sayings he must have made up, because they seem to
belong only to him:

If you don't stand for something, you will get knocked
down by everything.

Cooked potatoes are easy to eat, but you have to do some
gnawing to get meat off the bone.

There are no "little white lies." They are all black, trying
to hide from the truth.

When you become discouraged, think of the hole a little
ground squirrel makes in the side of the hill. It does not
bother him how large that mountain is.

Don't be concerned about something that don't concern
you. It won't make your bed any softer, or your meat fry any
faster.

Two things I love to hear, but seldom do: truth and meat
a'fryin'.

I think the one he used most was "Devil take it." He told
about the one time when he came in from picking blackberries without his shirt. His mother asked him why he had
no shirt and he answered, "Well, you see, I kep' git'n caught
in these blackberry briars. And ever'time I would say, 'Devil
take it,' and I guess the Devil, he just come and took it."

CHAPTER TWENTY

SARAH ALVERTA WAS my sister's name but I always called her Sissy. She was born with a normal mental capacity, but when she was eighteen months old, she had a fever that lasted six weeks. The doctor called it a brain fever. When she recovered she could not talk and her mind never grew anymore, but remained as the mind of a two year old. She might have been taught some if she had had the right teacher. We ourselves could have done more for her, if we had been rash with her; but we loved her so much we gave her her way in everything. The whole household was run to suit what we thought was best for her. My sister Vada was the one who loved her the most and took constant care of her, sleeping with her at night, washing her clothes, even diapers.

She was a few years older than me, but I soon learned that whatever she wanted of mine, I was supposed to give her. I did not resent this because I had been taught that she was someone very special. I remember once I had a fried egg in my plate and she reached with her hand and took it and ate it. I thought it was a big joke and laughed.

Once we were playing near the chair shop where my father was making chairs. The little nobs or ends of wood that were left as scraps from the ends of the finished chair post, made very nice playthings. With a child's imagination they could become anything from a father and mother with a whole family, to a table covered with pots and pans. To me they could be anything. All Sissy liked to do was beat them together to make a loud noise, or pile them up in a large heap and then kick them over.

I can remember many happy hours playing with Sissy and these wooden scraps. But what I am going to tell you next was told to me by my father.

He heard a loud noise, looked out, and found me pulling and tugging at Sissy. She was hitting me and kicking but I would not let go. Both of us were screaming and crying.

My father came running and parted us and demanded, "What are ye doing? Ye know ye must never fight with Alverta."

"But, Papa," I said, "There was a big worm. It might bite Sissy."

He went back to where we had been playing and he found a large copperhead, which he killed.

We did not get much candy, but each time my father went to the store he always brought back three large red and white peppermint sticks of candy, which were called "saw logs." There was one for each of us: Alverta, Edna, and me—the youngest of all the kids. Sissy wouldn't eat candy. I don't know if she just did not like the taste, or if it hurt her several decayed teeth. But she loved the red and white striped color, so she always wanted one, mostly to play with. My father would always tell me, "Now don't ye take Alverta's candy, but ye watch her and when she gets tired of playing with it, you can have it to eat." I would follow her around for hours, and sometimes wait until she took a nap, but sooner or later, I got her candy.

Alverta loved anything that was red. One Christmas my sister Vada got a large apron, which was then known as a coverall. It was something like a sleeveless dress that opened up and down the back. The color was a bright red with a small, springly, flowered design. Alverta fell in love with it at once and Vada cut it up and made a dress for Sissy. She had this pretty red dress on that Easter morning that had such a sad ending.

Several boys had met in the large "bottom" or meadow just across from our home at the mouth of Trace to play a game of "round town," a game somewhat like baseball. Lots of girls had come to watch from our porch and yard. Everyone was having a good time. It was Easter and everyone had on their new clothes for the occasion.

When we heard a terrible scream, everyone ran in the house and found Alverta's clothes on fire. Lorenda ran for the water bucket, which was empty. Vada began tearing at the burning clothes, but before Renda could get a bucket of water from the well, all Alverta's clothes were burned.

My father had just been gone for a few hours on his way to Wheelwright, where he had a job as a "planer" in a carpenter shop.

Someone sent for a nurse who stayed at the Caney school. Someone said, "Who will go overtake Isom?" Hazy Caudill said, "I have the fastest mule, so I will go."

In my childish trusting mind I thought "everything will be alright again, when Papa gits here." The next thing I remember was running to meet him, when I saw him coming, and he hugged me until it hurt. I did not know until later that he had been told I had been the one who got burnt.

Sissy lived until about midnight. I can still see my father

as he pulled the sheet up over her head and told the nurse,
"It's over."

CHAPTER TWENTY - ONE

I REMEMBER THE first time I ever heard of Mrs. and Mr. Lloyd, who founded the center and school that are now Alice Lloyd College. My father and Frances had gone to the corn crib and shucked two "coffee sacks" full of corn for the next mill day. Alic Jacobs had a mill house. He had built a dam across the creek to catch the water. The power of this water, when the gate was opened, would turn the large millstones and grind the corn into meal. In payment for this service he took part of the corn for himself. There was a kind of wooden dipper called a "toll dish," a small one for his portion of one-half bushel, and a larger dipper for a full bushel. Each man's corn was ground in turns, depending on his arrival. (I guess this is where we got the nickname a "turn of meal," meaning a sackful.) This gathering of a group of men was enjoyed by all. It was a time to catch up on all the news, and enjoy a lot of joking and laughing. Every young boy thought himself grown-up when he was allowed to go to the mill.

All the women took great pride in seeing how nice and clean their meal sack looked. Some would stitch their name or initials on the sacks so as not to get them mixed up. Others, who did not like to sew, would tie their sack with colored string. These meal sacks were of very heavy material, a cream color with a small red or blue stripe running lengthwise along each side.

This particular time Papa and Frances came back from the crib with the corn. Renda went to the quilt shelf and got a clean quilt. After sweeping the floor and moving everything out of the way, she spread this large quilt on the floor, and Papa poured the corn on top. Father and the older girls placed their chairs around the corn, close enough so that they could pull the edges of the quilt up over their knees, somewhat like an apron. Then they began to shell the corn, letting the grains fall onto the quilt. The smaller kids sat on the floor around the edges and shelled too. Sometimes Papa would have to start ours for us by shelling two rows of grain. This was called "rowin' it."

We would throw the cobs in a pile in the corner of the room to be used later for fuel to burn in the grate or cook stove. After a while the younger ones tired of working, and anyway, by that time there were enough cobs for us to play with. Edna would place them on top of each other in the form of a square that looked a lot like a log cabin. When it was very tall, she would let me or Sissy give it a push, to watch them all tumble down. Sissy loved to do something like this. Sometimes we would build houses, fences, and roads. We had just as much fun with our cobs, as children now do with electric trains and tinker toys.

After a while I began to listen to the grown-ups talk. Renda said, "Did you know Bish Johnson went over on Reynolds Fork and got them strange people, who come from off yonder, to come here on Caney to live? He give them some of his land, if they would come over here. Why do you think he did that Paw?"

"I don't know fer shore, but it may be fer the best," Papa answered.

"I can't see why they want to come here. Some people think she is goin' to bring in teachers. If she does, our own teachers will lose their jobs."

"Well," Papa said, "let's wait and see. Don't try to judge the other feller until ye know all the facts."

Then Frances said, "Well, some people think they are working for the government and will find out where all the moonshine stills are and report them to the revenuers."

Edna looked up and asked, "Well, Papa do ye guess these strange people believe in God like we do?"

And my father answered, "Well, I think everyone in the whole world believes in God. These folks don't believe exactly the same beliefs we do, but they have promised to not interfere with our religion, politics, and our moonshine stills."

Everyone was silent for a few minutes; then Frances spoke up and said, "Some of my cousins at school said Mrs. Lloyd has been givin' people some clothes and things, not new store-bought clothes, just old clothes."

Renda said, "'Lo, I would not want to wear somebody else's clothes, if I did not know whose they were. Why, they might be dead people's clothes."

"Or even been wore by some old nigger," Vada said.

Father said, "Vada, why do you hate niggers so?"

"I don't know; just 'cause Granny Frankie did. You know Granny said a nigger did not have a soul like white folks do."

"Your Granny did not believe that. She just talked to hear her head rattle. A nigger is just like anyone else; some good, some bad. I would druther be a black man with a white soul, than a white man with a black soul."

Renda said, "You know all I can remember about Granny Frankie is: one day I asked her why the rusty spots were on the Rusty Sweet apples and not on other apples, and she said, 'Nature.' And when I asked her what nature was, she answered, 'Hair on a nigger's nabble, that's nature.' Granny shore loved to joke."

By this time all the corn was shelled. My father made a three-cornered opening by catching the edges of the meal sack with his teeth and both hands. Renda got a plate from the shelf and using it as a shovel, she scooped the corn up from the quilt and placed it into the sack. Then she folded the quilt and put it back in the shelf. While they were doing this, Edna and Frances had put all the cobs into an empty coffee sack and placed it behind the stove.

Soon, we were all in bed asleep.

•

I shall never forget one Christmas when I was about five years old. I had been looking forward to the holiday eagerly, ever since Preacher Billie had gone from house to house all up and down Caney Creek, even to the very head of each hollow, making a list of everyone's name and age. We had all been promised a "Christmas gift" from the Center school.

Even all the baking and stewing and cooking of all the good things to eat, did not make as big an impression as the thoughts of this package soon to be mine. I talked about it by day and dreamed about it by night.

At last the day before Christmas arrived and Father went to get our gifts. It seemed like hours and hours before he returned with two large bags with his name in big letters and a "Merry Christmas from C.C.C.C." written on one side.

We never even thought of waiting any longer, but tore into the bags at once.

Inside were smaller packages in bright colored wrappers,

one for each member of the family. As luck would be, mine was the last, the very bottom one in the bag.

It was a large brown package tied with a heavy twine. I was so eager to get into it, I tried to break the cords. All the other girls were busy with their own, and were shouting, "Look what I got."

My father soon came to my rescue and cut the strings with his knife, and I hastily dug in. I will never forget, until my dying day, what I saw.

It was the remains of a large faded brown teddy bear, no eyes, one ear gone, a dangling leg, and a mangy-looking covering from which the straw stuffing was protruding in more places than one. I gave one look, threw it on the floor, and ran screaming to my father's arms for comfort. I think the angry look on his face frightened me more than that hideous monster. In a voice I had seldom heard from him, he said. "Well, I guess them folks from off yonder think we are in a hard place to think a little child would be tickled with a thing like that for Christmas."

He threw the whole thing, wrapping string and all, into the fire. My enjoyment for Christmas that year was not completely restored even with the poppa doll and cap-pistol he had bought for me.

In all fairness I must say I don't believe anyone connected with the school had anything to do with this. I believe they had sent it on to me, wrapped as it was, from "our good friends" up north. Mrs. Lloyd herself sent me another present when she heard of my bear. I do recall a new silver quarter, which was doubly precious; she had "sent me word" that this coin was a present to me from her.

CHAPTER TWENTY - TWO

I THINK ONE of the best times I can remember is "eating around the fire." Sometimes it would rain and we'd be caught without dry wood for the stove. Sometimes it would just be cold and the girls would "dread" to cook in the kitchen. Then they would get us something to eat by using the fire in the grate.

They might make mush, which is cooked in a large kettle hanging from an iron bar fastened to the cracks in the chimney-rock, high above the fire. Water, to which a little salt has been added, is brought to a rolling boil. The cornmeal is slowly poured in with one hand, while you stir it constantly with a large spoon in the other hand. You have to be very careful or the mixture will get lumpy. But if made just right, it will be of a very mushy thickness. This is then dipped out in spoonfuls into your bowl and covered with milk—a very delicious meal.

Maybe it would be beans or fresh meat the girls would cook in the big iron kettle. Sometimes they hung it from the iron rod or placed it directly on the grate. Then the bread would be baked under the grate in the hot cinders. You have never in your life eaten anything that tastes as good as corn bread baked this way. You add a little soda and salt to cornmeal and just enough water to make a thick paste. The skillet must be preheated and the inside covered with a small layer of lard or grease. This is so the bread will not stick to the skillet.

The fire must not be too hot. The cinders under the grate are hollowed out to form a place for the skilletful of dough. Some folks put a lid over the skillet and then knocked more hot coals on top; I prefer to let it bake without a lid. Maybe a few cinders did fall into the dough, but what did that matter? They could be picked out, and anyway, a child is supposed to eat one peck of dirt in its lifetime.

We would sometimes roast sweet potatoes, Irish potatoes, apples, and eggs under the grate in the hot cinders. The eggs had to have a small hole made in them and a straw stuck in the hole. This was to keep them from bursting or exploding when they got hot. If they did burst and got a few ashes or cinders on them, we just rubbed it off and ate the eggs anyway.

Of course there was always a big supply of popcorn. Every family owned a big long-handled wire "popcorn capper." If you pop corn over a fire made from burning willow wood, you get a flavor in the corn from the burning willow that is very good and different from anything with artificial flavors you buy now in the markets.

We also parched the regular white corn, normally used for feed or meal. To parch corn, you shell it first, then you put it in a skillet containing a large spoonful of lard or butter and a small amount of salt. The skillet is kept real hot, either on the stove or grate, and the corn must be stirred constantly. It becomes very brown and brickle, and very good.

We always gathered a large supply of nuts to be eaten during the winter: black walnuts, chestnuts, and hazelnuts, or "hazenuts" as we called them, to name a few.

In the summertime there were always plenty of berries and apples. And in the spring when the sap or watery liquid began to form under the bark of the trees, we would tap the "sugar trees" and get a sweet woody tasting drink. But I think the most fun of all was to "go sappin'."

My father would take his ax and we would each have a spoon. We would climb the hill until he found just the right-looking birch tree (you could also use beech, but birch is much better). My father would cut the tree down and then take the bark off in large slabs by cutting rings around the tree about every two or three feet. Then he would split the bark between the rings and it would come off in two large half-circle pieces. The inside of this bark had a very juicy lining, which we scraped out with our spoons and ate. Some people added sugar and let it sit overnight, but we most always ate ours there in the woods.

There was also a small, thick leafed plant with red berries that grew close to the ground on the tops of hills, which we called "mountain tea." We gathered and chewed the leaves and ate the berries. There were some roots of plants we also ate as a snack, like "sweet anise" and "pop paws."

There is a tree that blooms real early in the spring. It has beautiful white flowers and later, a small red berry that we used to eat. I don't know what the real name of this tree should be, but I do know why we mountain people called it a "sarvis berry."

Back in the early days we had no church house and people lived so far apart that the only religious connection with a church was the "circuit rider" preacher: a preacher who rode all over two or three counties, up hollows, and across the hills, stopping to stay a few days at someone's home where he performed a service. All the neighbors would gather at this house to hear him. There would usually be a few couples of young people that had been waiting for him, so they could get married. He would also preach a funeral service for all folks who had died since his last visit. He had a certain time to visit a community. The time he was to come to our part of the county was in the spring when these "sarvis"—for service—berry trees were in bloom. The mountain people had no calendars back then, but when this tree began to bloom, they knew it was time to watch for their preacher.

My father used to tell a funny story about going with some young girls, about his age, to gather some of these sarvis berries. When they got to the tree they found that all the limbs were too high for any of them to reach. My father decided he would climb the tree, and, by swinging from the limbs, the weight of his body would bow the tree over, close to the ground. But the tree was very large and he was small, and the tree only bowed a little and left him hanging halfway between the top of the tree and the ground. He asked two of the girls to get hold of his feet and pull, so with their combined weight the tree would bend over. As no mountain girl would touch the body of a man before they were married, the girls got hold of his pants legs instead. Everything would have been just fine, but when they tugged his pants legs, his "gallous" (suspenders) broke and his pants fell off. Folks did not wear undershorts back then. The poor girls were so embarrassed that they dropped his pants and ran, leaving him to drop several feet to the ground.

Watching for the sarvis berry was natural when you hiked along the creeks like we did—we grew up close to nature and partook of all her changing seasons.

I remember how we used to walk—not like those "brought on" people who jog, trotting along like a stiff-kneed mule, their eyes looking straight ahead like they had been used to wearing a blind bridle, half-naked, their elbows sticking out like the wings on a picked chicken. I mean to need and want to go somewhere, and having no way to get there except on "shank's mare."

You get out early, while the ground is damp with dew. The sun is creeping slowly into the valley. You are in no hurry, so you take your time, just so you get home in time to do up the work before dark. You breathe deep the nice clean air, taking time to notice the odor of flowers, and to listen to the rejoicing voice of the birds. (That's the trouble with the world today; we just don't take time to enjoy ourselves with the entertainment God gives us free.)

As you pass each house you look to see if there is anyone you could holler at. All ask you where you are going. One woman says, "If you stop at the post office, please see if I got any mail." A man is building a fence. He is afraid he is going to run out of nails before he gets done. Would you please bring him a nickel's worth of eight penny nails from the store.

When you come to a place where the road crosses the creek, you place rocks in the water to step on. As you jump from one rock to another your foot slips and you baptize one of your feet. You laugh and look quickly to see if anyone saw you. Had it been winter you would have stopped at the next house, gone in and had a nice long chat, while you dried your shoe and sock in front of the fire.

Soon you come to a place where a woman has a fire built under a washtub. She is dipping up water from the creek to heat, so she can put out a washing. Again and again the road and the creek interwind, and you place more rocks to step on, jumping across when you can.

You meet a mother who is taking her children to see Grandma. She is carrying a baby in her arms and leading one almost as small. The largest boy has another little one on his back. The kids are very shy and keep hiding their faces in their mother's skirt as she talks a few words with you.

And then you overtake the school kids, noisy and still shining from their morning bath, shuffling along, walking in the dustiest part of the road, letting the soft dirt squish up between their toes, each swinging a bucket that once contained four pounds of lard, and now is full of "crumble in milk." The smaller boys and girls are in separate groups. The larger ones are walking in couples. By the time they get to school they will have walked off much of their excess energy and will be tired enough to set still and listen to what the teacher has to say.

We also walked to and from church, sometimes as much as four or five miles. A lot of nice, clean "sparkin'" went on in these walks. It's so nice to walk your best girl to church, no matter what age you are: just met, just married, or if you both walk with a cane.

You have been musing to yourself and would have passed the next woman, without speaking, an unpardonable slip of good manners, had you not heard her hoe hit a rock. She is hoeing her garden. You lean against the fence and discuss with her the wisdom of doing the cabbage first, waiting until the sun dries the dew from the leaves of the tomatoes and cucumbers.

There-is just one thing better than taking a walk along a country road, among folks you know and love—and that is going the same journey with a friend.

CHAPTER TWENTY - THREE

BY THE TIME I was about six years old, my father got a job making chairs for Mrs. Lloyd. About this time he "divided his land" and gave it to his children. My brother, Vince, got the "old home place."

My father bought a small "lot" or plot of ground from my Uncle Sam, near Alice Lloyd College. He built a "boxed" house made from sawed lumber, four rooms with lots of windows. It was very much in style with the changing times, but I loved our old log home much better.

Most of the chairs my father made were used in the school. There are still a few left now. He made lovely flower boxes or "fern stands"; I have two of these, and I see several yet in the home of my neighbors.

By this time all my older sisters had married and left home, one by one. There was just Edna and me still at home when we moved to the new house, and very soon after, she too was married.

For a while there was just Father and me. I remember this

as being the happiest part of my childhood. Looking back now, I know my father was having a very hard time taking care of me, with all the cooking and housework, after his day's work in the chairshop.

I stayed with one of our close neighbors from the time school let out until he got home from work.

Every few weeks he would take a wagonload of chairs to Wayland, to be shipped by freight up north. This was why he was so late getting home on this particular evening. It was summertime. There was going to be some "big doing" at the school that night. All the community had been invited to come. The neighbors, my baby-sitters, were busy doing their evening chores and getting supper ready. I crawled up in a big chair on the porch and went to sleep.

When the large bell was rung by someone at the school, telling everyone the show was about to begin, my friends forgot all about me in their hurry not to be late.

It was dark when I awoke all alone. I was so scared! There wasn't a light in anyone's house. Everyone had gone; not a soul but me in the whole neighborhood. I knew how to light the old-fashioned oil lamps, but I had never been allowed to use matches. So I just sat there in the dark and cried and cried. Oh how glad I was to see my father when he came to get me! I remember running into his outstretched arms. How safe I felt when he lifted me up and carried me all the way home.

As he put me in the bed he said, "Well, Junner, looks as if I am goin' to haft to git ye a stepmom to take care of ye, when I'm gone to work."

As far as my life was concerned, that was the worse decision my father ever made: not his wanting to marry, but in his choice of a second wife.

I know I was a spoiled brat. I had never been spanked, but was always petted and given my own way by my father and older sisters. But looking back now through the eyes of a grown-up, I don't see why she did all the things she did.

A code of the hills is "never to speak ill of the dead," and one of my father's sayings was, if you can't say anything good about anyone, don't say anthing "a'tall." But then I would have to leave my stepmother completely out of my story.

The first few weeks everything was just fine, but soon something happened to change that.

One day some older boys were going to take a mule and sled to get a load of apples from the orchard at the head of Sparkman Branch. All the younger kids, the ones who were about my age, were going along to help pick up the apples. I asked my father if I could go along. It would be a lot of fun and then, of course, they would give me all the apples I wanted to eat, even a bagful to bring home.

My father told me I could go if my cousin Denny went with us. That was another code of the hills. No female was allowed to go far from home without the protection of some male of the same family. They had this respect and reverence for their "womenfolks," even when they were very young.

For some reason, Denny did not go with us, but my stepmother gave me permission to go anyway.

When I came home my father met me at the door very angry and demanded, "Why did ye go atter I told ye not to, if'n Denny didn't go?"

"But Barbara said I could," I told him.

"Well, she told me she didn't," he answered.

I had always been taught to tell the truth. I had never lied to my father in my life. I looked at my stepmother and said, "You know you said I could go. You know you did."

She looked me straight in the eyes and said, "No, I didn't."

I turned to my father and said, "Believe whichever you

want to, but you can ask the other kids; they heard her."

I think he knew who was telling the truth. I don't think he bothered to ask anyone else. A few days later he told me that I did not have to "mind" my stepmother, but to always get permission from him when I wanted to go somewhere.

I wasn't allowed to touch anything that belonged to my stepmother. Even worse, if I wasn't there when she and my father ate, everything was thrown out and I got nothing to eat.

I remember well the night when things finally came out in the open. I guess—looking back now—my father had noticed a lot, and was just hoping everything would work itself out.

We did not own a cow then; my stepmother could never learn to milk. Each evening after school I walked up to my sister Renda's home on Short Fork to get a small bucket of milk, which she gave us. I was having so much fun playing with her children that I forgot it was getting late. At last Renda came to the door and said, "Ye better go, honey. Paw will be worrying about ye if ye are atter dark git'n there."

So I got my bucket of milk and ran almost all the way home. Sure enough, they had eaten and gone to bed.

My father grumbled a little at me and told me to hurry and eat and get to sleep.

I went into the kitchen and looked, but as always there was nothing left from their supper. I put the milk away and slipped into my bed.

My father heard me and said, "Now don't be all mad because I quarreled at ye, and not eat any supper."

I told him, "I am not mad, I looked and there weren't anything to eat."

"Ye could have drunk some of the milk with corn bread."

"But there weren't any corn bread," I answered. "I looked fer some."

"I know there was some left. I didn't eat all I wanted myself, so as to leave some fer ye. What did ye do with it Barbara?" he asked my stepmother.

She did not answer him, so he got out of bed and went to look for himself. He found it in the bucket of scraps, that was saved for the pigs.

"Barbara," he said, "why did ye throw out everything? Ye knowed Verna Mae had to have something to eat?" This made me forget my fear of my stepmother and gave me courage enough to tell him, "This han't the first time; she does it all the time."

"Put ye clothes back on. Ye are goin' to have supper tonight," he said. I did not know what he meant, but I did as he asked.

He took me across the road to where Joe Jones had a store, which was still open.

"Now buy anything ye want to eat and I'll pay fer it." I did not have to be told but once, and I don't remember what I got, but to "eat out of the store" was a treat.

He and Barbara must have had a big quarrel, or racket as we say, for she moved out and they stayed separated for over six months, but they got back together after a while. Maybe she promised to treat me better, but by that time I had learned to stay out of her way. My father saw I always got something to eat after that. But she never would do anything for me.

As I got older my relationship with my stepmother did not improve, and finally, I just quit home altogether. I stayed with different folks; my father would pay for my board and I went to school. At last I went to the Center school to stay.

Mrs. Wheeler ran a kind of boarding house, called "Practice House," for girls. It was connected with the school in many ways, yet we were kind of a separate home. There were about ten or twelve of us. We had to obey all the rules Mrs. Lloyd had made. We were not allowed to have boyfriends, not even to walk along the campus with a boy. We had to wear white pleated skirts, long-sleeved middy blouses, long white hose, and white flat-heeled oxford slippers. The girls of Practice House did not eat at the school dining room, "Hunger Din."

We paid ten dollars a month. Some, like myself, paid cash. Others brought vegetables and fruits from home.

Mrs. Wheeler taught us to cook and keep house. She was a very strict and stern old lady. We had to obey her. I don't think any of the girls ever got close enough to her to ever like her very much. But you had to admire her. We secretly called her "Big Chief."

I loved my home at Practice House, but eventually it closed. Mrs. Lloyd made room for Mrs. Wheeler and us girls in her already crowded dormitories. I was placed in the downstairs of the girl's old dormitory, a place with such small rooms and little heat, that we gave it the nickname "Pig Alley."

Mrs. Lloyd got most all of her teachers from outside the mountains, or as we say, from off yonder. Some were good and came with kindness and understanding in their hearts, wanting to help. Some had formed their opinions about us from what they had read before they came.

One such person was a lady whom I will call Mrs. Parks, because I don't want to use her real name. She was a large, pompous woman, who's very walk seemed to say "God made me of better material than he did you, and I was privileged to be born up north."

She was in charge of the dining room. Four or five of us girls worked for her cleaning up the tables and washing the dishes. She was always telling us how to walk, how to talk—

to be a lady like her. The advice was great, but it was the way she went about it and the way she made us feel—so cheap—not any of the girls liked her.

One night something had happened on the creek, a bit of news that I knew the whole school had heard. Everyone was being very nice about it, not saying anything to me.

But not Mrs. Parks. I was at the last table in the very end of the room, when I saw her coming toward me.

She began asking questions about what she had heard. At first I tried to answer as politely as I could, without really telling her anything.

She was determined to know all the details. When she said, "Well, I don't see why the law does not do something about it," I looked her right in the eyes and answered, "You need not have any fear Mrs. Parks, for as low as these women are, they would not have anything to do with your husband or son. They hold themselves above that."

Letting her breath out in one big "humph," she wheeled around and started marching back toward the kitchen. One look at that retreating back and my anger overcame me. I let fly one of the plates I had stacked up, at her broad backside. As the plate crashed at her feet, she turned in time to dodge the second. Then she began running as, one by one, I threw all twelve plates at her, before she made it to safety inside the kitchen door. She was no lady then. Neither was I.

I went to my room and did not attend classes that day. I was almost sure I would get expelled from school. That evening when I was called to Mrs. Lloyd's office, I went expecting the worst. But her words were, "Why, Verna Mae, why? This is just not like you at all."

"Well, Mrs. Lloyd," I answered, "she was talking about my folks, and I have always been taught that you don't talk about anybody's folks to their face."

I am almost sure I saw a twinkle in her eyes, but all she said was, "Go back to your room. We will do something about it."

I was not punished in any way. I was given another job and someone else helped with the dishes.

Miss Cline showed us how to be a lady by being one herself. She was a small birdlike woman with red hair, which she always wore cut real short and straight. She taught French and Sunday school and played the piano. She introduced me to my first cup of tea, a habit that I still enjoy. I know you grandchildren will always remember the green mug that I drink my tea from.

CHAPTER TWENTY - FOUR

I LOVE TO think that the name hillbilly was derived from our way of talking, that "billy" meant William, because we still retain the words and expressions used by William Shakespeare.

The outsiders did not seem to realize that they sounded just as different to us as we did to them. We could understand them better than they could understand us, because we have so many quaint expressions that are meaningless to anyone but ourselves.

I remember a Mr. Moorehouse who taught history in high school. We were discussing the "Lost Colony" of Roanoke. I said, "No one knows what went with them," a mountain expression meaning that they were lost. When we don't know where something is, we say, "we don't know what went with it." I know it sounds very funny to a stranger. Mr. Moorehouse laughed and made me explain, which was all right.

He must have been a native of New England. He had a

very funny northern accent, and he talked through his nose.

Maybe he had embarrassed me, or I might have just "had a mean spell on me" that day, but the next question he asked me, I answered by using his same tone of voice, saying all the words so much in an imitation of his way of talking that all the other students in the room burst into a loud laugh.

Did that man get mad! He really ruffled me up good and put me out of the room by dragging me by my hair, but what hurt most was what he said.

"I would love to look your father and mother in the eyes. I would like to know something about the parents of a girl like you."

The next day school had just turned out when my father was returning from the post office, after delivering the mail. He was riding his mule and carrying a pistol as all mail carriers are required by law to do.

My father had some of the school children "point out" Mr. Moorehouse to him. After learning who he was, he rode his mule up beside him and stopped.

"Are ye Mr. Moorehouse?" he asked.

"Yes, I am. What do you want with me?"

"Well, first, I want ye to look me straight in the eyes." Mr. Moorehouse looked up. My father had his gun in his hand by then. When the teacher saw this, he turned very pale.

"Well, ye said yesterday ye would like to look into the eyes of Verna Mae's paw and maw. Well, ye are looking at her paw; her maw's dead. I had it in mind to give ye a good whoppin', but seein' ye are an old man (my father was past sixty-five at that time) I don't want to hit ye any. But ye get up on that rock wall and start runnin', not walkin'. And ye run every step 'till the end of that wall."

After the big washout or flood of 1927, when over half of the school had been destroyed by high water, Mrs. Lloyd had a wall built of split rocks from one end of the school to the other, as a protection against the future flood waters. This wall was about four-feet high and about two-feet wide.

Mr. Moorehouse took one more look at my father's face and the gun in his hand, and he climbed up on the top of the wall and began running. My father had to make his mule go real fast to keep up with him. Of course, everyone was laughing, fit to burst, except Mr. Moorehouse.

When he got to the end of the rock wall, my father put his gun back in his pocket and said, "Now I think we're about even. Ye go on about ye own business." And my father turned around and went home.

Mr. Moorehouse went directly to Mrs. Lloyd's office and told her what had happened.

She listened quietly until he was through talking, and then she said, "Well, my advice to you is to leave Caney at once. Don't stay until tomorrow. Pack your things and leave your address; I will ship them to you. Walk across the hill and go out by way of Hindman. I know Kitteneye, and he loves his children. We must remember, although we are here to help these folks, this is their home. We are the intruders."

CHAPTER TWENTY - FIVE

FOR MANY YEARS my father drove a wagon and brought the mail from Wayland to Pippa Passes. Mrs. Geddis, the mother of Mrs. Lloyd, was the postmistress for many years. She did not keep the office open from eight until four, as is done today. She stayed in her own room—a building quite some distance on the hill above the post office. She came to the office only when she was needed, which wasn't very often.

My father and Mrs. Geddis became very good friends. I think she had more understanding of us folks than anyone else from the outside. I know all the older folks loved her more and thought more of her, than other outsiders.

One evening, when my father came in with the mail, he hollered to her, "Oh, Mrs. Geddis, mail boy." She must have been very busy at something, with a lot of noise in the room. He called in a still louder voice, "Mrs. Geddis, mail boy." Finally she came to her door and said, "Oh, Kitteneye, do you want me?"

"Why, Mrs. Geddis, ye know I do. I been a wedder so long, I would take anybody I could get."

She understood that he only said this as a joke and meant no disrespect to her. She enjoyed the laugh as much as he did.

The mail wagon, going to and from Wayland, was our only connection with the outside. My father did many errands for the school and the folks who lived on Caney. It also served as a bus. Folks coming in or going out rode in his "jolt wagon," and the twelve miles in that wagon was no pleasure trip. He took folks to the dentist, doctor, or to catch the train for a longer trip, and brought folks back, coming in.

Everyday someone was sending him to get something from the drugstore, or other business, for things our small stores did not carry. He only received fifty cents a day from the government for his job as mail carrier, but the dimes and nickels that folks gave him for these little extra jobs helped to boost his income. Each rider gave him twenty-five cents as fare for the ride.

On one such trip, Mrs. Geddis sent him to the drugstore for some medicine for herself. At the same time, one of the teachers sent for some medicine for her pet cat.

That evening when my father delivered the packages to Mrs. Geddis, she asked him what she owed him for his trouble. He answered, "Ye don't owe me anything fer your medicine. I never charged anything I did fer a sick person. But I want a dollar fer that cat medicine. I think if some fool can give five dollars fer medicine fer a cat, she can give me a dollar fer bringin' it. There are too many little children on Caney that need medicine, than to waste it on a cat."

I never saw my father drunk in my life. My older sisters said that they knew he got drunk when he was young, but up until just a few years before he died he always "took a sip or two of whiskey" every day. During the winter months, when he would be driving to and from Wayland, he would drink a little whiskey. He thought it would keep him warm. Of course it was against government regulations for him to drink on the job.

Several times someone sent in a report to the Post Master General. But they could never get anyone who could say they saw him drinking. So without definite proof, there wasn't anything the law could do about it.

Once a year a postal inspector visits each post office, and so my father was driving the mail wagon when he made this yearly visit. The inspector, rode from Wayland with my father, right in the wagon seat with him, all the way. By the time they arrived at the end of their journey, it was plain to see that Kitteneye had enjoyed his daily drink of whiskey. The inspector could not understand when and how.

All mountain folks loved to "put one over on the law." My father loved to tell how they had stopped at this old woman's house to get a drink of water. The inspector and the other passengers on the mail wagon had plain water, but the dipperful she had given my father contained good old corn liquor. The inspector went back to Washington without even knowing the truth.

It is hard for the outside folks to understand this disregard we have for law enforcement. It is not that we are not law-abiding people. My father would have been willing to give his life to protect the mail from robbery. Once he was almost drowned in his effort to save the mail, when his wagon and mules were caught in a flash flood. But he thought it wasn't any of the government's business if he drank whiskey while on the job. To him it was no more than taking an aspirin.

There were many teachers who came from up north to

help Mrs. Lloyd with her school. They all rode the mail wagon from the end of the railroad at Wayland to Pippa Passes.

My father with his quick insight to human nature quickly sized them up. Some of the ladies would be frightened to death at the thought of the ride along this strange road with a person whom they did not know. After all the false stories they had read about us, they did not know what to expect. He would always calm their fears by saying, "Now look a'here. Ye don't know me and I don't know ye, but I have seven girls of my own, and ye are just as safe with me as I hope they would be with ye paw."

Then there were the ones who sat as far away from him in the wagon seat as they could, as if they did not want to be close to him. He would tell them, "I know me and my mules don't smell so good. I work hard and I sweat and get dirty. But it's honest dirt and I'm not ashamed of it. I always say, it's no shame to get dirty, but it is a shame to stay dirty."

It was a long ride. About dinnertime he would stop his mules and feed them and eat his own lunch. He always tried to make this stop at the school house. If school was going on, that much the better. He had a nice visit with the teacher and also the use of their outhouse. He loved to see the look on the faces of his "brought on" riders when he told them they were welcome to use these hillbilly restrooms. Sometimes when he stopped he would give the reigns to his lady passengers and say, "Now hold these mules tight. Don't let them run away." Afterward, he would tell about it, "Those poor souls, scared to death, a'feared them mules would bolt. It would have took fire stuck to their tails to make them move once they stopped to rest."

I think he enjoyed it best when he would have several men teachers to bring as passengers. He would tell them a lot of tall tales: killings, robberies, murders, and ghost stories; so untrue that it was a wonder anyone would have believed him.

Afterwards he would say, "Ye can try to tell these people the truth about us mountainfolks and they won't believe a word of what ye tell 'em. They have already formed their opinion of us, before they leave home. Ye can tell them a passel of lies and they will eat it up like a gang of chickens eatin' corn."

Some came to help at the school and some had reasons of their own for coming to the mountains, like a young woman, who gave her name as Miss Johnson, although it was plain to see when she got off the train that it should have been Mrs. Johnson.

The twelve mile ride in that jolty wagon probably hastened the birth of her baby. It was born two months early, the night she arrived at the school. Mrs. Lloyd knew how some of the mothers on Caney would feel about having an unwed mother teaching their daughters. She told Miss Johnson she'd have to send for her folks to come and get her.

A few days later a man arrived, who said he was her father. True, he had the same bright red hair that the baby had, but he was not over three or four years older than the young woman. If she had said he was her brother, folks might have believed her.

I was not old enough to understand what some old folks meant when they said they feared the little baby would be got rid of before the Johnsons got home.

There was a little boy, who I will call Tiny Tim, who would be waiting by the side of the road every day. My father would always stop, and Tim would say, "Would you give me a chaw of baccer, Kitteneye? Give me and brother both a chaw."

"I han't got a chaw in the world," he would answer.

"I know that joke. Ye named ye left pocket 'the world,' but ye allus got some in t'other pocket fer me."

My father always gave little Tim some tobacco. Once a teacher from the north, who was riding in the mail wagon, disapprovingly said, "You shouldn't give tobacco to a small child."

My father answered, "Tiny Tim has just a few more months to live. Can't ye see he is dyin' of consumption? He has few enough pleasures in this world. His paw and maw both died less than a year ago. I laid them both out fer burial. No, I don't think a little baccer is goin' to hurt him."

My father had nothing but contempt for anyone who was conceited. He loved to "poke fun" at folks who "put on airs." The conductor of the train that met the mail wagon at the Wayland depot each day was such a man.

He was very large and my father's being so small made his imitation more funny than ever. It always drew a great laugh from the crowd of people hanging around the depot and Wayland Post Office.

Kitteneye would wait until the train turned and started back on its return trip. Then he would step up to his wagon, push his old ragged hat back on his head, pull out his watch in an exact imitation of how the train conductor had done, and then in a loud voice he would say, "All aboard, all aboard." Then in his own voice he would finish, "All that can't get a board take a slab."

CHAPTER TWENTY - SIX

A GOOD FRIEND of mine, an outsider from Oregon, once asked me, "Why do you like to live in a place where 25 percent of the children born die when they are infants?"

I began to wonder about that. It did not seem to me to be true. I counted all the births and infant deaths in my entire family—brothers, sisters, uncles, aunts, and my husband's family—and I only got an 8 percent average. I thought, well maybe we Slones are just healthy or extra lucky. Then I made a list of all the folks on Caney; even up each hollow and branch. This only came out to a 10 percent average.

Next time I saw my friend, I told him of my own survey, but he still held to his beliefs. Statistics at Washington, D.C., showed that we lost 25 percent of our children. I don't know where they got their records, because many of the women had their children at home by themselves; there was no official record. We were our own undertakers, so there were no official records of deaths until the last twenty-five or thirty years.

Most all the old folks had to use a family Bible record or an old school record for proof of their birth, so as to obtain their "old age pension check." This statistic may be true of all Eastern Kentucky as a whole, but I know it was not true of Caney.

Many people who visit us for the first time are surprised to find us so happy and carefree. They have formed a mental picture of us as sad and bitter people, confused with a life of hard work, and without pride or hope.

My father and his neighbors enjoyed life very much. They did not think of themselves as being poor and deprived. To them hard work was not a drudgery, but something to enjoy and share, a way to meet and work in friendly competition.

They got the same enjoyment competing with each other in hoeing corn, that folks get in playing baseball, swimming, or tennis.

It was not only in their work that mountain people competed. They ran foot races, pitched horseshoes, broad jumped, and had a form of wrestling, which they called "scufflin'."

My father was very strong for one so small. There was only one man he could not win out with in a scufflin' match: Jim Perkins, the father of our congressman.

Once when they were having a friendly tussle, Mr. Perkins threw my father in a way that burst a "risin'" (boil). It was on a part of his body that caused him to sit sideways in a chair. The pain was so much, my father forgot the other man was a friend. He almost scalped him by biting a large chunk of hair and skin. Mr. Perkins wore the scar for life, but it was all in fun. The next time they met, they scuffled again. My father could throw Jim, but he never could hold him on the ground. He said it was because the other fellow had a hump on his back. Maybe this was so or my father might have used this as an excuse to save his pride.

Election day was another highlight in our everyday lives. As far as the folks on Caney were concerned, the selection of who became our school trustee was most important. On election day there would be a lot of horse swapping. Some of the women would bring baskets full of gingerbread made with molasses and lots of eggs and spices. The candidates would pay for the bread and "treat" the voters.

My mother died before women were allowed to vote, but she always got very involved in each election. Once she was celebrating the results of an election by ringing her dinner bell. A neighbor, who was very disappointed in the election returns, shot the bell rope. My father climbed up the pole and tied the rope back, while the man was still firing his gun.

Someone once remarked to my father that he was unlucky because his seven daughters could not vote. He answered, "No, but I'm raisin' seven of the strongest democrats ye ever seed."

In the year 1928, one of Kitteneye's sons-in-law was murdered. He was the only witness to the crime. After the trial he quit his job as chairmaker for Mrs. Lloyd and moved to Dwarf. He wanted to avoid any trouble with the criminal's family.

He bought a small farm and built a house. He started a chair shop of his own and tried to sell chairs to his neighbors. These were the years of the Great Depression; no one had money to buy anything.

My sister Vada and her husband had moved to Virginia. My brother-in-law had bought a farm and worked in the mines. But the mines began laying off men. The ones who did get work, only got a few days each week. My brother-in-law could not meet the payments on his farm, and when he lost his home, my father wrote and asked them to come live with him. So they sold their livestock, loaded all their furniture in a truck, and started toward Dwarf.

The kids were riding in the back of the truck, very weary and tired, happy that they would soon be with Grandpa. They were almost there. As they were coming across the mountain at Sassafras, another truck began trailing behind them. The driver of the other truck was a black man, the first negro these children had ever seen. He looked very strange to them. They tried to get their father and mother's attention by shouting to them. The black man became angry. He hit their truck, causing it to go over the hill and into the river below. He drove off without even looking to see what he had done.

The driver of the wrecked truck was killed. All the rest were hurt. They were taken to a hospital in Hazard. One boy lost his hand, another his leg. My father asked the doctors for the child's leg, so he could bury it. He said it was his own flesh and blood and he did not want it treated as garbage.

I was staying at the Caney school when I heard of the accident. I went to Mrs. Lloyd and told her I was going home.

She said, "Are you asking for my permission, or are you telling me you are going?"

"I have to go," I answered. "These are my folks and they need me."

"You will lose a whole year's work."

"I know, but I want to go. Can I come back next year?"

"Sure, come back, your place will be waiting for you. Who will take you?"

"No one," I answered, "I will walk." It's twenty-one miles from Pippa Passes to Dwarf, and another mile to where my father lived on Bear Branch. I walked the whole way.

It was a long time before my brother-in-law was able to work. The hospital bill was large, and there was a depression going on. We all had to eat. My father decided the only way to get any money was to make moonshine whiskey.

Some bootleggers from Harlan had been trying to get some of the old-timers, who knew how to make the old-fashioned corn whiskey, to provide them with some. My father knew how to sprout the corn, grind it, and make real corn whiskey. Almost everyone had forgotten the old way, and used meal. I don't think my father did very much; I think he just taught the others.

In my yard grows a "bubby bush." I do not know the real name of this shrub. It has a dark purple flower, with a very pleasant smell. My stepmother's great-great grandmother is supposed to have brought the first one with her when she moved to Kentucky from North Carolina, many, many years ago. It is very hard to get one of these to live when transplanted. Maybe our climate is not suitable for it.

I had tried many times to bring one from my stepmother's yard, in her old home place, but each time it would die.

In the spring of 1946, my father brought me another sprout of the bubby bush. He helped me to set it out. He did not believe in any of the old superstitions, that so many of our mountainfolk do, but when he planted this flower, he said to me: "If this lives, I will die. If it dies, I will live." The bubby bush has lived for thirty-two years, and it blooms every year. My father only lived six more weeks.

INDEX

CPSIA information can be obtained at www.ICGtesting.com
Printed in the USA
LVOW06s0339301015

460409LV00001B/13/P